Hg2|Baku

A Hedonist's guide to...

Baku

Written & photographed by
Ben Illis

A Hedonist's Guide to Baku

Written by
Ben Illis

Photographed by
Ben Illis

Managing director – Tremayne Carew Pole
Marketing director – Sara Townsend
Design – Nick Randall
Maps – Amber Shields
Repro – Advantage Digital Print
Printer – Leo Paper
Publisher – Filmer Ltd

Email – info@hg2.com
Website – www.hg2.com

Published in the United Kingdom in September 2010 by
Filmer Ltd
Newcombe House, 45 Notting Hill Gate, London W11 3LQ

ISBN – 978-1-905428-46-5

Produced in conjunction with the Ministry of Culture and Tourism of the Republic of Azerbaijan

Ministry of Culture and Tourism
of the Republic of Azerbaijan

Hg2|Baku

How to...

A Hedonist's guide to Baku is broken down into easy to use sections: Sleep, Eat, Drink, Snack, Party, Culture, Shop, Play and Info. In each section you'll find detailed reviews and photographs. At the front of the book is an introduction to Baku and an overview map, followed by introductions to the main areas and more detailed maps. On each of these maps the places we have featured are laid out by section, highlighted on the map with a symbol and a number. To find out about a particular place simply turn to the relevant section, where all entries are listed alphabetically. Alternatively, browse through a specific section (e.g. Eat) until you find a restaurant you like the look of. Surrounding your choice will be a coloured box – each colour refers to a particular area of the Baku. Simply turn to the relevant map to find the location.

Book your hotel on Hg2.com

We believe that the key to a great Baku break is choosing the right hotel. Our unique site now enables you to browse through our selection of hotels, using the interactive maps to give you a good feel for the area as well as the nearby restaurants, bars, sights, etc., before you book. Hg2 has formed partnerships with the hotels featured in our guide to bring them to readers at the lowest possible price. Our site now incorporates special offers from selected hotels, as well information on new openings.

The concept

A Hedonist's guide to Baku is designed to appeal to quirky, urbane and the incredibly stylish traveller. The kind of person interested in viewing the city from a different angle – someone who feels the need to explore, shop and play away from the crowds of tourists and become part of one of the city's many scenes. We give you an insider's knowledge of Baku; Ben wants to make you feel like an in-the-know local, and take you to the hottest places in town (both above and under ground) to rub shoulders with the scenesters and glitterati alike.

Work so often rules our life, and weekends away are few and far between; when we do manage to break away we want to have as much fun and to relax as much as possible with the minimum amount of stress. This guide is all about maximizing time. The photographs of every place we feature help you to make a quick choice and fit in with your own style.

Unlike many other nameless guidebooks we pride ourselves on our independence and our integrity. We eat in all the restaurants, drink in all the bars, and go wild in the nightclubs – all totally incognito. We charge no one for the privilege of appearing in the guide, and every place is reviewed and included at our discretion.

Cities are best enjoyed by soaking up the atmosphere: wander the streets, partake in some retail therapy, re-energize yourself with a massage and then get ready to revel in Baku's nightlife until dawn.

Hg2 Baku author

Ben Illis

Ben's chequered past includes stints as an actor, writer, editor, photographer and book buyer as well as co-founder of Old Street Publishing. As a travel writer, he has written and edited for Frommers, Mr and Mrs Smith, The Style Bible, The Irreverent Guides and, of course, Hg2. He is rarely happier than when pounding the streets of a new city, camera in hand, or trekking through leech-infested rain forests in search of some obscure piece of wildlife, provided, of course, that there is a decent cocktail and some crisp sheets (high thread count, Egyptian cotton, natch) to crawl between as reward for all his hard work.

Baku

Baku is a city of enormous contrast. Phrases like 'melting pot' and 'East meets West' get used far too much in describing certain cities, but here in Baku the clichés really do ring true. This is very much where Europe meets Asia, where Muslim meets Christian, where the former Persian Empire meets the former Soviet one. Not a second passes in Baku where you are not reminded of all these different places, times and states and yet the whole adds up to produce a singular, unique, thriving, growing, fascinating and emotive mass that is far greater than the sum of its component parts.

Around the turn of the last century, Baku was in the grip of its first Golden Age. The oil was flowing, European families such as the Nobels and the Rothschilds were here making their first fortunes. Barely a soul on the planet had not heard of Baku, one of the richest cities on the planet, where, like California in the Gold Rush, any man could make good. Enormous, lavish, European-style mansions sprang up around the walls of the Old City, monumental extravagance was the order of the day for the sophisticated rich and Baku revelled in its hedonistic glory. Then, in the confusing aftermath of the First World War, came the Soviet invasion and seventy odd years of occupation did an extremely good job of wiping all trace of this desert town from the world's collective conscience, to say nothing of leaving a huge amount of sprawling, drab and concretey Soviet construction.

Now, however, not even two decades on from independence, the oil money is flowing once again and the second Golden Age of Baku is well under way. Old Soviet buildings – and sadly some crumbling but glorious nineteenth century ones too – are being torn down and replaced at a rate of knots. Towers of all shapes and sizes are shooting up all over the place, though quite who is going to occupy these myriad offices and apartments is anyone's guess. For inspiration, Baku has often looked to Dubai, its sister city in the black stuff, and to its big brother Moscow. No great surprise then that it is to these two cities – and notably Moscow in the 1990s and Dubai in the early 2000s – that Baku is in many ways most readily compared. Only time will tell if Baku is prepared to look at the mistakes these two great cities have made and avoid the problems that have blighted them both in recent years.

Ask any Bakuvian or long-term ex-pat how the city has evolved over the past five years and they will tell you that it is all but unrecognisable. Hotels, bars and restaurants are constantly opening up, demonstrating a far higher level of sophistication than encountered here for decades. Interior design is cutting edge and concept is all. The service industry is still young, so it would be churlish to expect the level of service of, say, London or New York. That being said, Azeri cuisine is rich and varied, international cuisine well-represented and foodies are extremely well catered for – even oenophiles are in for a pleasant surprise. Aficionados of luxury travel and especially shopaholics will find a lot more than they may have bargained for too, although they may on occasion balk at the price tag.

As desert cities go, Baku is remarkably green and its public space would put many cities in Southern Europe, for example, to great shame. Interesting to note too, that every ounce of the tons of soil required to develop the parks and green spaces of Baku was imported by ship. This was due to the efforts of the particularly forward-thinking Mayor R. R. Hoven, who passed a decree back in 1880, saying that every ship docking in Baku must bring fertile soil as ballast. Unsurprisingly, the amount of oil awaiting export was a great motivator and before long Mayor Hoven had all the fertile soil he could want and a grand expansion program of parks and gardens began.

No introduction to Baku would be complete without mention of The Caspian, the world's largest inland sea (or lake, depending on which school of geographic thought you subscribe to). Baku lies on the Absheron peninsula, which thrusts westward into the Caspian like the hooked beak of the stooping eagle, to which Azerbaijan's silhouette is often compared. The Caspian has about a third of the salinity of ocean water. This salinity gives rise to a unique biodiversity, with many of its endemic species, including the seven caviar-producing species of sturgeon, found nowhere else on the globe. The Caspian's water levels have always fluctuated and in Medieval times its waters were known to lap right up to the base of Maiden Tower. However, today, the level lies 28 metres below sea level, 3m higher than it was at its 20th century low in 1977 and the same as was recorded back in 1929. Unfortunately, the Caspian is seriously polluted with oil, but before the blame is laid entirely at the feet of irresponsible industrialists, we should bear in mind that oil has been leaking naturally from the sea-bed for millennia.

The Soviets were nothing if not lovers of fountains, statues and other grand chunks of monumental and public architecture. Ten years ago most of the public spaces had fallen badly into disrepair and not a single fountain worked in the city. In 2001 a huge city-wide clean-up was started including large-scale renovation works around city. This has resulted in noticeably fewer fountains and statues (and a lot of dust), but, when works are completed in May 2010, all will hopefully be revealed, restored and in full working order. A nocturnal stroll along the Boulevard taking in the gloriously illuminated, often musical, fountains is one of the great pleasures in what by night must surely be one of the world's most beautiful cities.

Of course in an expanding economy and a city to all intents and purposes this young, there are many more miles to go and an infinite number of directions this could all take. That's the excitement of being in a city like Baku at a time like this. Life here is sure as hell not straightforward and never easy, but there's unlikely ever to be a dull moment. For now, our advice would be to buckle up, hold tight and enjoy the ride, because things are moving on up in Baku… and fast.

Baku Overview

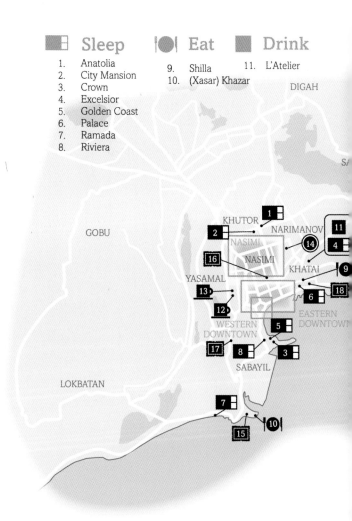

■ **Sleep** ●▮ **Eat** ■ **Drink**

1. Anatolia
2. City Mansion
3. Crown
4. Excelsior
5. Golden Coast
6. Palace
7. Ramada
8. Riviera

9. Shilla
10. (Xasar) Khazar

11. L'Atelier

DIGAH

SA

KHUTOR
NARIMANOV
NASIMI
NASIMI
GOBU
KHATAI
YASAMAL
EASTERN
DOWNTOWN
WESTERN
DOWNTOWN
SABAYIL
LOKBATAN

Snack Party  Culture

12. Baku Roasting Co.	14. Metkarting	15. Bibi Heybat Mosque
13. Chocolate Café (2)		16. Circus
		17. Martyr Hill
		18. Museum of Modern Art

ZABRAT

AZIZBEYOV

JCHU

BAKIKHANOV

IZAMI

SURAKHANI

SHARG

GARACHUKHUR

YENI
GUNASHLI

HOVSAN

Caspian Sea

0   5km

Old City & Western Downtown

The biggest and undoubtedly best cultural pull in Baku is the Old City, or Icheri Shahar, which was designated a UNESCO world heritage site back in 2000 and dates, in parts back to the 6th century. It is a higgledy-piggledy maze of tiny streets, lined with buildings of all ages studded with beautifully ornate, carved wooden doors and wrought iron-grated windows. Like a living museum, it is difficult to know where to point your camera as you wander around, gloriously lost, soaking up the rich atmosphere.

Public sculpture is a common sight all over Baku. In the Old City, it is worth mentioning the out-sized bust of the poet Vahid, situated in a leafy square by the Italian embassy just to the South West of the Shirvanshah Palace. Symbolic scenes from the work of the poet have been beautifully sculpted into his hair to great effect. Another unusual Old City sculpture can be found walking from the Meridian Hotel towards the twin gates which open on to Gala Street. Keep your eyes up on the roofline and you will find the famed Old City cats sculpture, together with the young boy and girl in their alcove below (above right).

Immediately to the West of the Old City wall lies the Old City metro – formerly Baku Soviet metro – with its controversial, Louvre-esque glass pyramid. A nearby bird-cage-like drinking fountain has twelve taps, each allotted to a sign of the zodiac (the eagle-eyed may spot that Aries and Taurus have been mis-assigned their spigots). Next to this is the impressive red brick and sandstone City Hall (Baku Soviet itself), recognisable by the Azeri flag flying over its towering domed gatehouse. The streets radiating North and Westwards from here are lined with stunning examples of crumbling late nineteenth century architecture, including the Palace of Happiness (see Culture). It is always worth keeping your eyes up on the roofline in Baku, so as not to miss some interesting and unusual architectural flourishes.

South from the metro along the Old City wall lie the splendidly laid out terraces of Filarmonia Park, also known variously as the Governor's or Gubernator's Park, with its fountains and groves of trees, filled with noisily chattering parakeets. Look out also for the unusual wall-mounted clock on the Old City walls, which is neon-lit by night.

The Filarmonia itself (see Culture) is an instantly recognisable yellow and white structure with domes, spires and arches aplenty. Diagonally opposite the Filarmonia lies the Presidential Office building, photography of which is strictly forbidden. Down the hill from this lie the two grand old buildings of the Mustafayev Art Museum (see Culture), while at the foot of the hill lies the impressively sized SOCAR (State Oil Company of the Republic of Azerbaijan) building and the rapidly ascending construction heights of the new Four Seasons Hotel.

Across the busy street on the Boulevard is a generously sized flagpole – though nothing compared to the new one being constructed at the end of the Boulevard extension to the West – and the pier to the Yacht Club, which is inexplicably guarded by rottweiler-like guards. The Yacht Club is a popular wedding venue and hangout for the city's newly wealthy, although apart from the water lapping round it has little else to recommend it. Boat trips depart from this pier and for 6AZN take about 40 minutes to circumnavigate the bay. A little further on is the impressive new International Mugham Centre (see Culture), whose organic silhouette is unmistakeable, especially when illuminated by night.

It is from here and to the South West that the Boulevard is being extended, which will give it the distinction of being the longest seaside promenade in the world, ending in what will be the tallest flagpole in the world. Above that is Martyr Hill (see Culture), most easily accessed by the old but renovated Soviet funicular railway, which lurches up the hill every twenty or so minutes for a mere 20 gapiks. It runs from 10am until 10pm. Behind Martyr Hill lies the iconic, nocturnally multi-coloured TV tower, which is the tallest structure in Azerbaijan and has a wildly expensive revolving restaurant up top, which is all but inaccessible to all but governmental invitees these days.

Old City & Western Downtown

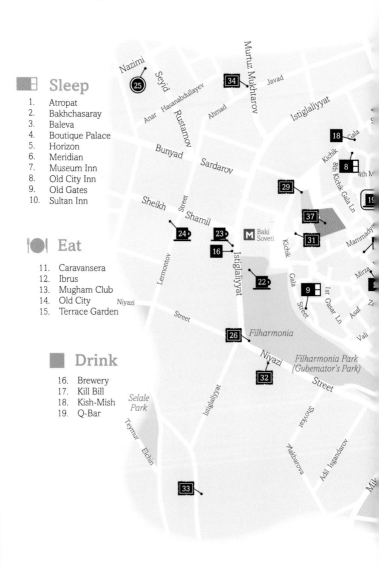

🛏 Sleep

1. Atropat
2. Bakhchasaray
3. Baleva
4. Boutique Palace
5. Horizon
6. Meridian
7. Museum Inn
8. Old City Inn
9. Old Gates
10. Sultan Inn

🍴 Eat

11. Caravansera
12. Ibrus
13. Mugham Club
14. Old City
15. Terrace Garden

Drink

16. Brewery
17. Kill Bill
18. Kish-Mish
19. Q-Bar

0   200m

Caspian Sea

Yatch Club

☕ Snack

20. Chocolate Café (3)
21. Chocolate Café (4)
22. Dondurma
23. La Vita
24. Pizza Holiday

◎ Party

25. Face Club

▦ Culture

26. Filarmonia
27. Hajinski Mansion
28. International Mugham Centre
29. Kichik Gala
30. Maiden Tower
31. Museum of Miniature Books
32. Mustafayev Art Museum
33. Open Air (Green) Theatre
34. Palace of Happiness
35. Puppet Theatre
36. Gyz Galasy
37. Shirvanshah's Palace

■ Torgova & Eastern Downtown

Torgova (pronounced Targórva) takes its name from the Russian 'Torgovaya Ulitsa' –meaning Trade or Commercial Street – the old Soviet name for the stretch of Nizami Street from Bulbul to Azerbaijan Prospekts. In Soviet times this was the main commercial drag of the city and remains so today. By extension, the name was applied also to Fountain Square and is still the best landmark for taxi drivers dropping off in the commercial centre of town.

As we go to press, Fountain Square is closed for extensive renovation – along with nearby Molokan Gardens and, indeed, much of the open spaces of the downtown area and even stretches of Nizami Street itself. A peek over the hoardings implies the end result, which should have been revealed by the time this book hits the shelves, will be very pleasant indeed.

To the South of Fountain Square, between the Old City walls and Molokan Gardens lies an area densely populated with ex-pat pubs, generally insalubrious basement nightclubs and hook up joints and some of the city's best restaurants. A few of these bars and nightclubs, including the popular Corner Bar and Crossroads nightclub, as well as the mother of all hook up joints, the Infiniti Club, lie across Nizami Street, clustered a block or two to the north of Fountain Square.

To the north, the streets rapidly decline in road surface and lighting until, just a few blocks from the glitzy centre, you will feel very much in a developing economy. While best avoided by night – due to bad lighting and mud-filled potholes as much

as any real danger – this area is where a lot of the untouched and enigmatic Victorian era buildings remain and should be explored, by daylight, if nothing else in search of the wonderful old Fantasia Hammam (see Culture and Play).

In the eastern corner of Fountain Square are the well known and much photographed Book and Art alleys in which stalls sell a surprisingly large range of discounted second hand books and some, er, 'curious' art, respectively.

Continuing East along Khagani Street a few blocks will take you to Sahil Park, after the nearby Sahil Metro, where some of the city's most stunning fountains are beautifully illuminated by night. The impressive building at the north-eastern corner of the square is the Akhundov Library (The National Library of Azerbaijan), with its statue-lined façade to rival that of the Museum of Literature. Akhundov was a nineteenth century playwright and philosopher, known as the Azerbaijani Molière. Further east along Nizami lies the Landmark (see Sleep) and the vast behemoth of Government House, or Dom Soviet, overlooking Azadlig Square and the Boulevard.

The Boulevard is one of the most European areas of Baku and, like a slightly faded English seaside resort, is awash with carts selling popcorn and candy floss, open air cafés, photographers, fair-ground rides and the like. At its Eastern-most point, near Government House, is the commercial port of Baku, which is still very much in use, although most of the commercial traffic will soon be routed to the new port

complex being built 40km to the south of the city. Near the port gates is the main concentration of fairground rides and a long curved stretch of seafront, masked for the most part by trees, where young lovers come for a kiss and a cuddle and a romantic gaze out across the sea.

Right in front of Government House, in Azadlig Square, an impressive array of fountains puts on a majestic display of almost acrobatic waterworks every evening with the illuminated seat of power forming a magnificent backdrop. From here, leading inexorably back towards the Old City and beyond, the path runs along tree-lined walkways and subtle landscaping, flanked by small cafés and refreshment carts, as well as yet more fountains and huge, ornate flowerbeds.

A large construction with a small gherkin-like tower at each end just to the east of the Boulevard's almost central pier is the new Boulevard Park centre, with shops, bars, restaurants, cinemas and even, according to some rumours, a hotel. It is due for completion in late 2010, so time will tell. From the end of the pier itself, the whole of Baku spreads out like an amphitheatre seen from the stage. Here the magnitude of the city's recent construction becomes extremely apparent. Near the foot of the pier, the wedge-shaped new business centre and the curious undulating concrete roof of the Mirvari Café (see Snack) form two sides of a sort of square, which contains an unusual tower-like structure, displaying air and sea temperature, as well as the time. Behind this is the colonnaded façade of the Museum Centre, the former Lenin Museum, now home to several museums, including the Carpet Museum (see Culture).

West of here the Boulevard stretches on towards its new extension. Highlights along the way including a rather dilapidated looking Ferris Wheel, a beautiful and quaintly old-fashioned carousel, the Bulvar Klub sports centre (see Play) and a strange network of water channels and fountains, which form a kind of kid's park, currently closed and dried out for, one would imagine, renovation. Just east of the Maiden Tower, the other attractively colonnaded building is the Puppet Theatre, beyond which things continue in the same vein right up to the Yacht Club pier, which pretty much marks the end of the old Boulevard and the start of the new.

Torgova &
Eastern Downtown

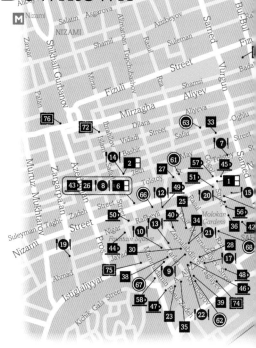

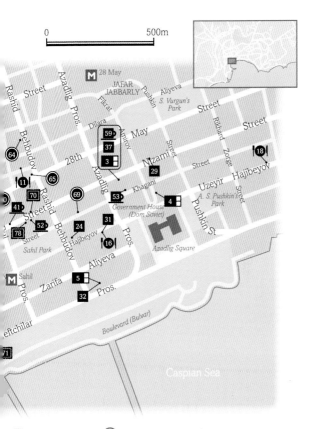

0 500m

Snack

40 & 41. Ali & Nino
42. Aroma
43 & 44. Azza Cafè
45. Balizza
46. Cafè Caramel
47. Cafè Mozart
48. Chocolate Cafè (1)
49. Dalida
50. Duplex Cafè
51. Fashion Cafè
52. Silvere Mask
53. Hazz Cafè
54. Marco Polo
55. Mirvari Cafè
56. Papillon
57. Shaorma # 1
58. Sunset Cafè
59. Vitamin Bar

Party

60. Black Jack
61. Crossroads
62. Indigo
63. Infiniti
64. Jazz Centre
65. Khalifa
66. Living Room
67. Pride
68. Studio 2
69. Twins

Culture

70. Opera & Ballet Theatre
71. Museum Centre
72. Fantasia Hammam
73. Heydar Aliyev Palace
74. History of Azerbaijan Museum
75. Museum of Literature
76. Azeri Drama Theatre
77. Russian Drama Theatre
78. Young Spectators' theatre

Nasimi

Despite being one of Baku's 11 official *rayons*, or administrative districts, ask any-one where Nasimi is and they will more than likely look blankly at you and assume you mean Nizami – named after the great 12th century poet from Ganja – and generally applied to the area surrounding the stretch of Nizami Street that runs alongside Fountain Square, aka Torgova. Just to further muddy the waters, Nizami is also the name of another *rayon*, but one bearing no relation to the location of either Nizami Street or Nizami Metro station, both of which are technically located in Nasimi – Nizami *rayon* is actually located some miles to the east of the centre. Confused? You will be. In actual fact Nasimi is also named after a poet, this time a 14th century Sufi one, and is a large area, centering on what is pretty much universally known as the Hyatt district. The main draw to the Nasimi district is the Heydar Aliyev Sports Palace, really more of a convention centre, home to the annual Oil and Gas Show, when Baku is at its fullest and prices have a tendency to rise city-wide.

Back in the mid 90s when Hyatt (see Sleep) built on their present site, this was an area of unprepossessing Soviet architecture. These days, the Soviet blocks have are being pulled down and are being replaced at a rate of knots by large-scale tower blocks of office and apartment space – though quite who the tenants will be for so much available, rentable space is anybody's guess. Many rather dilapidated Soviet blocks remain in between the dusty building sites and constantly evolving and changing lanes of traffic around Izmir Street.

With the arrival of a Western hotel chain, there was of course an influx of Western business travellers, with their Western expense accounts, and so many of Baku's better restaurants (all listed in Eat) are located in this area too: Scalini, Opera Lounge (see Party), Bibi and the Window group (all 3 restaurants meaning window in their respective languages) of Penjere, Mado and Finestra, to name but a few, as well as, of course, the Hyatt's in-house dining establishments. In addition to the Hyatt, the Grand Hotel Europe and the Ambassador have been pulling them in for years and so too will the all-new Qafqaz Point and Anatolia (all listed in Sleep).

To the south west lies the University district, centering around Huseyn Javid Square, home to the Baku Roasting Company and one of the more restauranty branches of the Chocolate Café. West of here is Yasamal, an upmarket residential neighbourhood, popular with long-term ex-pats, including a lot of diplomatic personnel. North east of Nasimi lies Ganjlik home to Baku's second set of golden arches and, more to the point, the truly world-class Sabun Nga Thai spa. Ganjlik has long been known as the diplomatic area, although in reality many embassies have now moved downtown and their staff spread far and wide. Pretty much due east of Nasimi is the Narimanov *rayon*, a middle-class residential neighbourhood and home to the tricky to find Metkarting club (see Party and Play) and all round pleasure palace.

Nasimi

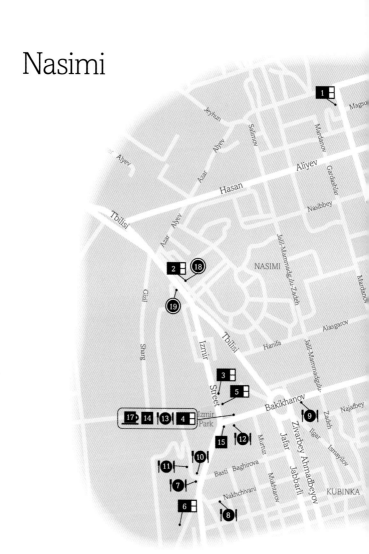

Sleep

1. Ambassador
2. Grand Hotel Europe
3. Hyatt Apartments
4. Hyatt Regency
5. Park Hyatt
6. QafQaz Pt.

Eat

7. Bibi
8. Finestra
9. Jasmine/Olive
10. Mado
11. Penjere
12. Scalini
13. The Grill

Drink

14. Beluga
15. The Lounge

Snack

16. Hayat Çay Evi
17. The Gourmet Shop

Party

18. Chevalier
19. Opera Lounge
20. Oscar Club

Culture

21. Azer – Ilme Carpet Factory

sleep…

The Baku hotel scene is seriously on the move. Firstly came the Landmark Hotel's ballsy, sleek and minimalist debut in 2009, which gave the others food for thought. Then, the old Soviet behemoths – The Azerbaijan and The Absheron – were torn down to make way for new names – The Hilton (opening 2010) and Marriott (2011), respectively – and the imminent arrival of these, and others, at the party has caused a flurry of the three 'R's – renovation, restoration and rebuilding.

The other big name new opening for 2011 is The Four Seasons, whose site on Neftchilar Prospekt and impressive graphic visualisations will surely make it one of the most prominent in town. Also slated for 2011 is a promising opening from the Turkish luxury chain Dedeman. Other grand and ambitious construction projects – such as the Full Moon and Crescent Moon – are also in various states of readiness and currently on the long-list for 2012 and beyond.

The original international players have perhaps been guilty of a little laurel-resting over the years, but the newcomers have really raised the bar and all are now in various stages of upping their game – the Hyatt is well into renovation of their Regency and Park properties, the Radisson Group is soon to follow suit at ISR Plaza – although their Park Inn and Sultan Inn properties are new enough already. The old Grand Hotel Europe is now under new ownership too, so presumed to be receiving an extensive makeover in the hopefully not too distant future.

The extension of the Boulevard to the south west has also opened up access to

the once rather isolated Crown and Riviera Hotels and has led to another imminent new opening on the luxury end of the scale in the shape of the Azeri owned Golden Coast, currently scheduled for early summer 2010. Other Azeri owned properties of note include the established lux-fest Excelsior and the all-new Qafqaz Point.

The vast majority of travellers to Baku are here for business and some company or other is inevitably picking up their tab, so prices are far from competitive and it is tough to find real value for money. Cheap beds in Baku are something of a contradiction in terms, although some 4 and even 3 star properties, such as the Anatolia, the Riviera and particularly the Hale Kai, perform better than others.

With a couple of exceptions – The Sultan Inn and, arguably, The Boutique Palace – true boutique hotels do not really exist in Baku. Many hotels, notably in the Old City, claim to be boutique but are, in actual fact, just small, simple guest-houses. These vary greatly in style and service and the best five are included here for those not on a corporate expense account, or who prefer a simpler pace of life.

Lastly, as many travellers are here for the long haul, we have included the best of the, admittedly limited, options for serviced apartments. Real estate agents will hook you up with un-serviced long-let apartments, our recommendation among these can be found in the Info section.

the best hotels

Top ten:
1. Sultan Inn
2. Landmark
3. Boutique Palace
4. Hyatt Regency
5. Excelsior
6. Golden Coast
7. Qafqaz Point
8. Hale Kai
9. Riviera
10. Museum Inn

Style:
1. Sultan Inn
2. Landmark
3. Excelsior
4. Qafqaz Point
5. Hyatt Regency

Atmosphere:
1. Sultan Inn
2. Excelsior
3. Boutique Palace
4. Landmark
5. Hale Kai

Location:
1. Sultan Inn
2. Museum Inn
3. Radisson Blu Plaza
4. Meridian
5. Boutique Palace

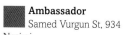

Ambassador *(top)*
Samed Vurgun St, 934
Nasimi
Tel: 449 49 30
www.hotelambassador.az
Rates: 180–550 AZN

The Ambassador Hotel is the flagship in the Azeri C-Group hotel chain and the only hotel in the group to have received a coveted 5th star. While rooms are comfortable and certainly of a generous proportion and the service is friendly and efficient, the décor is just a little worn and the hotel will no doubt welcome the renovation that is planned to take place over the next year or so. Sadly, however, no amount of renovation can do anything about the hotel's position, which, at the rather non-descript northern end of Samed Vurgun Street, leaves it, we feel, just a little bit out in the cold for the majority of travellers. However, if circumstances require you to be in the area, the Ambassador is certainly a hotel that merits consideration.

Style 7, Atmosphere 8, Location 7

Anatolia *(middle)*
Yusif Vasirov St, 108
Ganjlik
Tel: 564 14 75
www.hotelanatolia.az
Rates: 120–180 AZN

The Anatolia is a brand new 4 star opening and an impressive addition to the range of upper mid-class hotels in Baku. Rooms are large and decorated in cool shades of blue and silvery grey, with dark wood headboards and furni-

ture. Perhaps more impressively, they also possess some of the biggest plasma screens this hedonist has ever seen! Although one would hope you have travelled to Baku for more than just a TV. There is a small, but reasonable fitness centre with indoor pool and all the usual business facilities of a Baku hotel. As with its big sister The Ambassador, however, it is really only position that lets the Anatolia down, located, as it is, in an even remoter and uninteresting district near Ganjlik metro than its sister property.

Style 8, Atmosphere 7, Location 6

Atropat *(bottom)*
Magomayev St, 11-13
Old City
Tel: 497 89 50
www.atropathotel.com
Rates: 180–325 AZN

Named after the eponymous pre-Christian ruler of Atropatena, the region that came to be Azerbaijan, the Atropat opened its doors in January 2008, offering a good, solid 4 star service in the heart of the Old City. A new build, tastefully completed in a similar style and tone of sandstone to the original buildings of the Old City, The Atropat is not bound by an original layout like many hotel conversions in the Old City, so rooms are generally larger and, in the case of the suites, very generous indeed. The décor is opulent, although one can't help but feel that the cream woodwork and black and silver soft furnishings of the rooms and suites would be better served without the red and gold striped signature wall or

sleep...

rather migrainous carpet.

Style 8, Atmosphere, 7 Location 9

Austin *(left)*
Nizami St, 58
Torgova
Tel: 598 08 12
www.austinhotel.az
Rates: 177–260 AZN

Just a few paces off the stretch of Nizami Street formerly known as Torgova – i.e. shopping central – the Azeri owned Austin Hotel has been quietly plying its trade for five years. Located above shops and a lawyer's office, on the third and fourth floors of an original nineteenth century boom-town mansion, the hotel is an oasis of four-star calm, well-insulated against the noisy bustle below. The 31 rooms are decorated in various muted, tranquil colour schemes and the suites especially are very generously proportioned. All rooms have balconies overlooking Nizami Street. There is a small but reasonably equipped fitness centre and a restaurant offering breakfast and a small room service menu only, but with all the restaurants of downtown on your doorstep, you'd hope not to have to take advantage of that.

Style 8, Atmosphere 7, Location 9

Boutique Palace *(bottom)*
Aziz Aliyev St, 9
Torgova
Tel: 492 22 88
www.boutique-palace.com
Rates: 195–495 AZN

The nineteenth century mansion that is home to the Boutique Palace Hotel was not always attached to the 12th century Old City Wall. During the Soviet invasion the building was bombed and heavily damaged. In the resultant renovation the 1896 mansion – unusually for a Baku hotel originally built as a guest-house – was joined to the older wall that has become one of its most notable features. Its 10 suites are each named after a prominent figure in Azeri history, with portraits and biographies of said figure in place. They are tastefully decorated in a distinctly Orient Express style. Then there's suite 11 – The Sultan Suite – a kitsch explosion of infinity mirrors, rainforest showers, giant plasma screens and light projections that Austin Powers would be proud of and even features a giant fish tank and its own personal hammam.

Style 8, Atmosphere 9, Location 9

Crown *(right)*
Neftchi Gurban Abbasov St, 7
Bayil
Tel: 491 02 27
www.crownhotelbaku.com
Rates: 245–420 AZN

Sandwiched between the fun and funky Riviera (see page 50) and the brand new and lavishly opulent Golden Coast (see below), it is perhaps no surprise that the old school and unrenovated five-star Crown retains something of a solid, post-Soviet feel. That said, the rooms are of a comfortable size, the classically elegant décor is pleasant enough, the sea views are lovely and the service is efficient, if not exactly warm. The top floor restaurant has a good, solid menu and an expansive view out over the bay towards central Baku. The basement fitness centre with swimming pool is of a high standard and popular with guests and non-residents alike and yet still something just isn't quite right. Maybe it's the 3 week-old copies of the FT at reception?

Style 6, Atmosphere 6, Location: 7

 **Excelsior** *(bottom)*
Heydar Aliyev Ave, 2
Khatai
Tel: 496 80 00
www.excelsiorhotelbaku.az
Rates: 250–3,500 AZN

Entering the 330 square metre, 10 room Imperial Suite at The Excelsior, it is no surprise that this is the suite of choice for Russian rock stars when they play Baku. This suite is so vast, even the hallway has its own hallway. Fabulous roll top chaise longues and silk-canopied day beds; glittering chandeliers and Deco statuettes abound –there's even a baby grand piano (white, natch) for them to bang out their latest rock ballad. But fear not, for many of these features (piano excepted) are repeated, albeit on a slightly lesser scale, in the suites available to mere mortals. Perhaps surprising then that the standard rooms are done in such restrained, while still opulent, good taste. Also more than worth a mention is the fantastic Aura wellness centre – one of the most impressive hotel fitness centres we have ever seen.

Style 9, Atmosphere 9, Location 7

Golden Coast *(right)*
M.Huseynov, 14
Bayil
Tel: 491 52 00
www.goldencoast.az
Rates: 210–1,800 AZN

Lying at the Western end of the new Boulevard extension, due to open in early Summer 2010, The Golden Coast, also opens its doors in early summer (inshallah) and is the latest glitzy offering on the buffet of the Baku luxury hotel scene. Here, space – and opulence – are the name of the game. From the marble-floored, palm-lined reception to the Louis XIV style furniture in the golden-domed, er, Golden Bar, you know this is one place where less certainly does not equal more. Rooms are very generously proportioned and, while the carpets tend perhaps a little towards the bright, the décor is certainly luxurious. One lovely little detail is the electronic touch pad Do Not Disturb sign, so you can live out a brief Star Trek gadget fantasy before collapsing back into the Ottoman Empire and the deep feathery heaven of your bed. The outdoor terrace bar and restaurant has great views over the Caspian and back to Baku too, though the kitchen is not yet open, so the food remains untested.

Style 9, Atmosphere 8, Location 7

Grand Hotel Europe *(left)*
Tbilisi Ave, 20
Nasimi
Tel: 490 70 90
www.grand-europe.com
Rates: 200–600 AZN

sleep...

Not so long ago the Grand Hotel Europe sat glittering in all its sparkling blue and white orientalist glory, perched lustrously atop a hill conveniently right next to the Sports Palace – really more of an exhibition centre and home to the annual Oil and Gas Show. These days, however, the sparkle has dulled somewhat and the Europe stands a little cracked and forlorn, dreaming of better days. The rooms, of course, are still large and the views nothing short of spectacular, but the atmosphere is woefully lacking. The latest news is that the American owners have sold to an as yet unnamed Azeri group and a major refit is set to take place. No schedule for this yet, but we shall definitely be watching this particular space with great interest.

Style 5, Atmosphere 7, Location 6

Hale Kai *(top)*
Mirza Ibrahimov St, 18
Torgova
Tel: 596 50 56
www.hotelhalekai.com
Rates: 130–160 AZN

Baku is filled with places you wouldn't expect to stumble across and chief among them must be the American-owned Hale Kai (Hawaiian for 'home by the sea') decorated throughout in homage to American architectural design legend, Frank Lloyd Wright – think wonderful stained glass panels, signature high-backed chairs and other ingeniously functional built-in furniture. All mod-cons are covered, including a well-stocked vodka bar at reception – try and get past the owner without being bought a drink! This is also one of the few hotels in Baku to have commissioned an accurate tourist map. Staff is well-trained and the service is far better than one might expect from the 3 star rating. If you need to speak to someone about accessing some of Azerbaijan's wilder landscapes for a memorable weekend away, then they are the ones, as the owners maintain some off-roaders at a camp in the mountains and plans are afoot for a more extensive mountain-based eco-resort – watch this space.

Style 8, Atmosphere 8, Location 8

Hyatt Regency *(bottom)*
Bakikhanov St, 1
Nasimi
Tel: 496 12 34
www.baku.regency.hyatt.com
Rates: 240–1,480 AZN

When the Hyatt Regency first opened its doors back in 1996 it enjoyed a brief monopoly on the business travel market. As other chains have opened the Hyatt has been forced to up its game and has responded in style. As we go to press, the Regency renovation is all but complete and the results are stunning. Rooms are done out in subtle shades of muted greys, mauves and creams and create a relaxed, sophisticated atmosphere. The communal areas also shine, with The Grill (see Eat), The Gourmet Shop (see Snack) and the Beluga Bar (see Drink) all making the grade for inclusion in these hallowed pages. And, of course, if the Regency is looking this good, we can only wait with bated breath to see what is done with the Hyatt's flagship brand the Park Hyatt, whose renovation is also set for completion in 2010.

Style 9, Atmosphere 8, Location 8

 Landmark *(top)*
Nizami St, 90
Torgova
Tel: 465 20 10
www.thelandmarkhotel.az
Rates: 200–250 AZN

The Landmark Hotel's arrival in February 2009 marked a serious raising of the bar for the international players on the Baku hotel scene. Located at the top of the prestigious, pink granite Landmark office building, offering stunning views across the bay to the hills of Sabayil and the omnipresent thrust of the TV Tower. Rooms are generously proportioned and all about pared down, sleek, minimalist lines, which are even more successfully employed in the hotel's communal areas and the fabulous Sky bar (see Drink). The Landmark's health centre is also one of the best gym facilities in town, with the excellent Vitamin Bar (see Snack) and a sun deck with views to die for. As we go to press, construction continues with a two floor restaurant extravaganza to crown the hotel due to open in the early summer of 2010.

Style 9, Atmosphere 9, Location 8

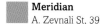 **Meridian** *(right)*
A. Zeynali St, 39
Old City
Tel: 497 08 09
www.meridianhotel.az
Rates: 215–385 AZN

The Meridian Hotel (no relation to Le Méridien group) has enjoyed surely one of the best locations imaginable since its opening in 2003. Indeed, it has become such a landmark that it is oft-quoted in directions when trying to locate somewhere in the maze-like streets of the Old City. It is something of a shame, therefore, that for a five-star hotel the rooms feel a little, well, four-star. Space is definitely not an issue – especially in the suites – but the décor has seen better days and if the Meridian is to keep up with the new openings over the next few years, then one can only hope that the renovations that are being discussed as we go to press take place sooner rather than later. The hotel has good facilities, however, and its proximity to the excellent restaurants and sights of the Old City is a huge bonus.

Style 7, Atmosphere 7, Location 9

 Metropol *(left)*
Hajibeyov St, 33-35
Torgova
Tel: 598 19 10
www.metropolbaku.com
Rates: 175–290 AZN

There's something about the Metropol's bold colour scheme of red and black with dark metallic silver curtains which feels a bit like a late 80s gangster's den, but it certainly works. Rooms are large; fittings are well thought out, with plasma screens et al throughout, and the ultra-complicated space-age multi-jet shower cabinets are, well, complicated! Under the same ownership as the soon to be opened World Fashion Lounge next door (on the site of the

much-missed former Taboo and Yin-Yang restaurants), the Metropol offers an affordable slice of grade B rock star luxury in a part of town that's particularly convenient for the Boulevard and the Landmark-led business district that's sprung up around Government House, but that's also only a few blocks stroll from the shops and services of Torgova and the Old City.

Style 8, Atmosphere 8, Location 8

Museum Inn *(bottom)*
G. Mahammad St, 3
Old City
Tel: 497 15 22
www.museum-inn.az
Rates: 160–200 AZN

Right next to the Sultan Inn, overlooking the excavated *caravanserai* of the Old City and with an equally magnificent view across the Maiden Tower to the Caspian Sea beyond, The Museum Inn has a more homely feel to it and a personal, if slightly chaotic, style. The reception area and bar is an explosion of colour and texture, with some interesting features, including an original and (very) deep well and some stunning antique painted chests. Standard rooms are not the biggest – well this is a converted nineteenth century mansion, so the architects had to make do with what they had – but the fittings are comfortable and the top floor suite, complete with a lovely private balcony, more than makes up for it on the space front. The communal balcony is a wonderful spot to breakfast too, secluded and comfortable and with that stunning view.

Style 7, Atmosphere 8, Location 9

Palace *(right)*
Khatai Ave, 39
Khatai
Tel: 496 92 57
www.ayf-palacehotel.com
Rates: 170–960 AZN

Located around 10 minutes by taxi to the east of the city centre, although conveniently on the airport road, the Palace Hotel is housed in a glorious nineteenth century mansion that perfectly suits the classically elegant style within. Rooms here are large and decorated in a traditionally refined European style, with shades of cream set against dark wood furniture and, in some rooms, elegant glass-fronted display cabinets of fine bone china. The overall effect is all very Parisian, although with a welcome Azeri accent. The service is extremely friendly and efficient and the view from the rooftop bar makes it worth a visit for a late night tipple, although perhaps not worth the trek for non-residents. It's just a shame though that the hotel is located in a rather unexciting part of town.

Style 8, Atmosphere 8, Location 7

Park Hyatt *(left)*
Izmir Street, 1033
Nasimi
Tel: 490 12 34
www.baku.park.hyatt.com
Rates: 320–1,800 AZN

As we go to press, Hyatt's flagship brand – The Park Hyatt – is undergoing a major refit to bring it into a posi-

44

tion to compete with the myriad new luxury hotel openings scheduled for Baku over the next few years. As things stand, this grand dame of the Baku hotel scene is showing her age somewhat. However, if the newly completed renovations at Hyatt's second brand, The Regency, are anything to go by, once completed in late 2010, The Park will have seriously upped her game and be ready to take on all-comers. For now though, while service is very much among the best to be found in Baku, the out-moded décor does do her down a little. Part of the refit, incidentally, is an all new health and spa centre – we shall be watching this space with great interest.

Style 7, Atmosphere 8, Location 8

 Park Inn *(bottom)*
Azadlig Avenue, 1
Torgova
Tel: 490 60 00
www.baku.rezidorparkinn.com
Rates: 199–269 AZN

Maybe it's just us, but there is something about the Park Inn's primary colour-based design palette which we find about as relaxing as a pneumatic drill outside our bedroom window at 7am on a Sunday morning. If, however, you would rather go down the 'shades of Mondrian' allusion route, then the Park Inn may just be for you. Service is friendly and efficient, the rooms are well appointed and of a generous size and, best of all, there's the exclusive Mirvari Club restaurant and bar (see Drink) with just about our favourite night-time view of Baku up on the top floor. This 3rd outing for the Radis-

son/ISR Holdings partnership – they are also behind the Radisson Blu Plaza and the fabulous Sultan Inn (see Sleep) – does come across as the most mass-market of the group's estate, but that's no accident, because it is and, as such, very successful it is too.

Style 7, Atmosphere 6, Location 8

 Qafqaz Point *(top)*
Kazimzade St, 118
Nasimi
Tel: 510 78 78
www.caucaspointhotel.net
Rates: 240–450 AZN

The newest opening for Azeri hotel group, Gilan Tourism, The Qafqaz Point (sometimes also listed as Caucas Point) is their first urban hotel, sitting alongside their seaside and other rural resorts. 74 rooms, kitted out to a very high spec, with all the usual mod-cons, contemporary design and a very generous amount of floor space throughout. The basement fitness centre is well-equipped and offers a range of facilities and treatments, while the Panorama restaurant and terrace bar offers a different angle across Baku's magnificent night-time skyline, as well as a good, solid, if perhaps a little unimaginative, menu. The hotel's tucked away location near the Hyatt business district can be tough to find, but crucially they will hook you up with a taxi firm that knows them well and only employs drivers who won't take advantage of foreigners on the fare.

Style 9, Atmosphere 8, Location 7

Radisson Blu Plaza *(left)*
Nizami St, 69
Torgova
Tel: 498 24 02
www.radissonblu.com/hotel-baku
Rates: 320–350 AZN

Back in the 90s, The Radisson was the second international hotel group to open in Baku and set up its flagship at the top of the iconic ISR plaza, just to the north of Fountain Square. As at hotels across the city, the imminent arrival of several high profile new five-star players has led to a fevered rash of renovation, and here we have to say, it is not before time. As we go to press, the hotel's impressively proportioned rooms with stunning views over Fountain Square to the Caspian beyond are looking very tired. However, if the newly renovated reception area (pictured) is anything to go by, then The Radisson will soon be vaulting its way up the charts and comfortably back into our top 10. Radisson has also teamed up with another ISR partner, the excellent Azza group, to offer an excellent bar (see Drink) and café (see Snack) and a very reasonable restaurant too (see Eat).

Style 6, Atmosphere 7, Location 9

Ramada *(top)*
Salyan Highway
Shikhov Beach
Tel: 491 73 03
www.ramadabaku.com
Rates: 200–1,500 AZN

20 minutes or so down the Salyan Highway to the south east of Baku and, crucially, towards one of the main oil drilling areas of the region, The Ramada is a sleek and impressive looking wedge of modern architecture right on its own private Caspian beach. Facilities are, as one would expect, top-notch, with a gym, two restaurants, indoor and outdoor pool, tennis courts, and a sports bar with billiards as well as, of course, access to one of the few coastlines in the world where you can top up your tan in 40+ degrees with an oil rig shimmering on the horizon – a curious experience any self-respecting hedonist should be only too happy to notch up. Rooms are large and comfortable, if a little sparsely decorated. Do try and book a sea-view, however, as the inland version is dreary in the extreme.

Style 7, Atmosphere 7, Location: 7

Riviera *(right)*
G. Abbasov St, 1
Bayil
Tel: 491 10 10
www.riviera.az
Rates: 145–210 AZN

With 20 rooms each done out in a different opulent style the four-star Riviera offers a slice of affordable rock star extravagance right at the south-western tip of the all new extended Boulevard. It's a bit of a hike into town, or a short cab-ride, and at times the location does feel a little isolated, but once you've sunk into the luxurious beds, you are unlikely to mind. Room 207 (pictured) is the one with the in-room Jacuzzi, but all are comfortable, if perhaps not as hedonistically inclined. Worth asking for a sea-view, if available, as the rooms that look across the city are nothing like as spectacular and can be a little noisy. The hotel restaurant and bar have splendid views back across the city, although serious foodies should definitely brave the journey into town for a far superior dinner.

Style 8, Atmosphere 8, Location 7

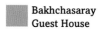 **Sultan Inn** *(top)*
Boyuk Gala St, 20
Old City
Tel: 437 23 05
www.sultaninn.com
Rates: 250–275 AZN

Nestled in the heart of the Old City, just above the Maiden Tower, The Sultan Inn is arguably Baku's only true boutique hotel. The hotel is located in a nineteenth century mansion and has just 11 rooms, all with open fires and tastefully decorated in dark wood with sumptuous chocolate brown velvets and gold highlights. Limited floorspace is amply compensated by a clever split-level floor design, so your bed chamber looks down over your cosy, romantic fireside seating area. Service is impeccably discreet and every detail has been taken care of to make your stay as pleasant and relaxing as possible. Up on the roof is an excellent restaurant – The Terrace (see Eat) - and the Q Bar (see Drink) which share one of Baku's best terrace views over the Maiden Tower and rooftops of the Old City to the Caspian.

Style 9, Atmosphere 9, Location 9

Guest Houses

Bakhchasaray *(left)*
Guest House
Mirza Shafi, 9
Old City
Tel: 492 87 20 (reservations to Museum Inn on 497 15 22)
Rates: 120 AZN

Run by the Museum Inn as a secondary guesthouse property, the Bakhchasaray features just four rooms in a narrow period property in a charmingly secluded, leafy Old City square. So charming, in fact, that it's no surprise that it's almost always full and we were unable even to get back into the rooms for a photograph! Rooms come in two sizes here – slightly smaller ones are located on the street side of the building, while very much more spacious ones with balcony and a view over the square towards the sea are towards the front. If there is availability, it is worth requesting the larger ones. Rooms are clean and simple – indeed, some might argue they are overly simple and could use a little more decoration – but if it's a quiet location right in the middle of the Old City you are after, The Bakhchasaray guesthouse is hard to beat.

Style 6, Atmosphere 8, Location 9

Baleva *(right)*
Sabir St, 12
Old City
Tel: 437 21 15/88
Rates: 140–165 AZN

A guesthouse that is a cut above the rest,

the Baleva has a handful of rooms in a stunning tall, slender townhouse overlooking a small cobbled square in the heart of the Old City. As with all hotels in this category, don't expect anything ultra-deluxe, but do expect things to be good, simple and clean. Rooms are airily decorated in light colours with interesting black and white photographic prints of Baku and around Azerbaijan. They do also vary in size, so ask for one of the rooms situated at the end of the building that overlooks the square, as these have small balconies and a few extra square feet of floor space. The staff at the Baleva is young, friendly and personable and very happy to help you out with restaurant reservations and the like.

Style 6, Atmosphere 7, Location 9

Horizon *(top)*
Mirza Mansur, 62
Old City
Tel: 418 44 01
www.thehorizonhotel.biz
Rates: 100–180 AZN

Perched on a quiet and secluded hilltop in the maze-like centre of the Old City, The Horizon Hotel has been quietly plying its trade since 2004. Although simple and decidedly on the shabby-chic side, what stands out here is a combination of space, service and an ever-so charming slight eccentricity. The 12 rooms are generously proportioned and decorated, as befits rooms named after some of the UK and Ireland's best golf courses, in a vaguely olde worlde, British colonial style – think dark wood furniture, framed prints and so on. Pleasingly kookily, a

couple of slightly battered, but remarkably comfy, old Marks and Spencer sofas have even found their way into the mix – don't even ask how they found their way to the Caucasus! Service here is friendly and little touches like complimentary bathrobes lift the Horizon out of the also-rans and into the ranks of the worth-knowing.

Style 6, Atmosphere 6, Location 9

Old City Inn *(bottom)*
Kichik Gala St, 16/10
Old City
Tel: 497 43 69
www.oldcityinn.com
Rates: 70–100 AZN

Most of the small hotels in the Old City claim to be boutique and most are, in fact, really more hostel than anything else. The Old City Inn may lack the upmarket design features of a true boutique hotel you might find in any European capital, however, it more than makes up for that in personal service. Small original features such as stone fireplaces lend an authentic period feel and matching upholstered headboards and cushions offer a pleasant, homely touch; while wandering around the higgledy-piggledy corridors of this old mansion will knock even the best sense of direction for six. Some of the rooms have a curious view over chaotic backs of buildings and roofs bedecked in laundry and satellite dishes to the Caspian too – more interesting than strictly beautiful, but it is a joy to have a balcony in the stultifying summer heat.

Style 7, Atmosphere 7, Location 9

Old Gates *(left)*
Kichik Gala St, 8/1
Old City
Tel: 497 87 23
www.oldgateshotel.az
Rates: 100–150 AZN

The one thing that marks the Old Gates out against the competition in the guesthouse category is space. The standard rooms are of a very reasonable size and the suites are frankly enormous. As is the case with many of the guesthouses the décor takes minimalism to the levels of spartan, but you're not really here to stare at the walls are you? And, in the dizzying heat of summer, you'll be very glad of all that extra air to circulate in your room. All suites include a sitting room, kitchenette and guest bedroom and the executive suites also have a third decent sized double bedroom. The Old Gates is conveniently located on the South Western edge of the Old City, just below the Shirvanshah's Palace Complex and a short skip from Filarmonia Park and the Old City Metro.

Style 6, Atmosphere 6, Location 9

Apartments

City Mansion *(middle)*
Azadlig Avenue, 153
Nasimi
Tel: 436 10 41
www.felsbaku.com/citymansion
Rates: 80–110 AZN

Set back a block or so from the northern end of Azadlig Avenue, and away from the noise of this rather busy thoroughfare, the City Mansion is actually a small grouping of several renovated blocks, now turned into serviced apartments. Available for long or short term lets and for as little as a night, they are

set around a small, tranquil garden at whose centre lies a waterfall, gently trickling into a pond full of impressively sized koi carp. Owned by the Singapore-based Keppel group, the Asian influence is felt in more than just the fish pond, as the acceptable, if not overly exciting, restaurant also serves a predominantly Chinese menu. Apartments here are of a livable size and standard, although nothing special, and the friendly staff available 24/7. There is also a fitness centre with indoor pool and a reasonable gym.

Style 5, Atmosphere 6, Location 6

Hyatt Apartments *(right)*
Bakikhanov St, 1
Nasimi
Tel: 496 12 34
Rates: 3,420–7,080 AZN pcm,
min one month rental

Not content with sewing up the international hotel market back in the 90s, Hyatt continues to make Baku one of its most successful locations by cornering the growing market in luxury serviced long-let accommodation. Around 90 serviced apartments and duplex villas, which share use of the hotels' pool facilities and their all new health club, opening in 2010, as well as all the other restaurants, bars and cafés of the Hyatt estate. An ongoing project, the Hyatt serviced apartments and villas are located in the Hyatt Towers adjacent to their main hotel properties. With very high-end modernist design, all mod-cons, high tech facilities and a full range of services, they are already proving to be among the most sought after addresses for long-stay ex-pat Bakuvians.

Style 9, Atmosphere 8, Location 8

55

eat...

A guide-writers worst nightmare, Bakuvian hostelries like to do their damnedest to be everything to everyone, so many of the venues in this chapter are as much (or almost as much) bar as café as restaurant and could arguably serve as well in the drink, snack or even party sections as they do here. Some also have menus offering a variety of cuisines. In general, we have tried to focus on what they do best and so you will be more than assured of a good meal at any of these places, especially if you stick to the cuisine for which they are mentioned, and, in many cases, you may also elect to stay on for some drinks after your repast.

In terms of dining venues worth a look mentioned elsewhere in the book, Gümüs Maska (Snack), The Face Club, and The Opera Lounge (Party) stand out. These latter two come in at the pricier end of the scale and both are at venues that are better known for their parties than their fine dining, however the Face Club's Nouvelle Cuisine is superb, as is the European menu especially at Opera. Japanese is also good at Metkarting (see Party). Poised to open any day as we go to press and also expected to raise the dining, drinking, lounging and partying bar significantly is The Chinar Lounge (see Party), from the same team as our current favourite Zakura. Chinar is an all-new multi-functional space, set in a renovated old tea house near the foot of the funicular railway that leads up to Martyr Hill. It will remain a tea house by day, effortlessly segueing into an Asian fusion restaurant and late lounge by night, staffed by a team imported from London's Michelin-starred dimsum joint Hakkasan. The tea theme is continued throughout and even features strongly on the menu, as well as, intriguingly, the cocktail list.

Azeri national cuisine is varied and very good, with noticeable nods to the traditions of Persia and Turkey, especially, but also elsewhere in the region. Famous

The Grill

national or regional dishes include *dushbara*, a mutton broth with small ravioli like filled pasta twists; *plov* (pilaf) is a dish of buttered rice accompanied by a stew or other meat or fish dish, usually served on the side. *Qutab* (Gutab) are rather like Mexican tortillas, served hot, folded and filled with spiced meat or greens; *kükü* are a little like a Spanish tortilla, often served cold, *dolma* can be used to refer to any stuffed vegetable, though the Greek-style vine leaf is prevalent; while *lavangi* are little bite-sized rolls of meat or fish, stuffed with an assortment of mouth-watering fillings. Azerbaijan is also, of course, one of the world's centres of caviar production and the black stuff features, at a premium, on many national menus.

All imported ingredients and wines are subject to an eye-watering import tax, so national food tends to be far better value for money. On the wines, Azeri wine-production is on the up and the results – especially among the reds – are really very palatable indeed. Do be careful and make sure you order a dry (Russian – *sukhoi*) red, as the sweet and semi-sweet (*sladki*, *pol-sladki*) options are a little like blackcurrant cordial and don't tend to sit well with a Western palate. Some wine shops for off-license sales are also listed in Shop.

As mentioned in the introduction, Azerbaijan is a country new to the service industry, so be aware this is not London or New York and try to exercise a modicum of

Caravansera

patience. Even if English is not spoken well, staff will normally be able and happy to help. Be aware though, that an apparently affirmative smile and/or nod is not always a guarantee that your waiter has understood your request.

Many cuisines are well-represented in Baku, notably Azeri, Georgian, Italian and Japanese, with good options also for Chinese/Thai, German, Korean and Lebanese all listed in this chapter. Indian food is available, but not in any great style. Your best bet for a curry is Adam's Bar (see Drink), while burger and tex-mex aficionados should head for The Sunset Café and pizzaholics to Pizza Holiday (see Snack).

Many restaurants offer a cut-price, fixed menu 'Business Lunch' on weekdays. This may seem like a great way to munch your way round the best of the best on a budget, but be aware that many restaurants rest their better chefs at lunchtime and even, in some cases, serve a different cuisine in the daytime. It is always advisable to call ahead and check.

Zakura

the best restaurants

Top ten:
1. Zakura
2. Occo
3. The Mugham Club
4. Old City Restaurant
5. The Grill
6. Mesa Lounge
7. Mosaico
8. Scalini
9. Penjere
10. Bibi

Food:
1. Old City Restaurant
2. Zakura
3. Occo
4. The Grill
5. Bibi

Service:
1. Zakura
2. The Grill
3. Occo
4. Mosaico
5. Aristocrat

Atmosphere:
1. The Mugham Club
2. Caravansera
3. Scalini
4. Mesa Lounge
5. Zakura

Aristocrat *(left)*
Samed Vurgun St, 23
Torgova
Tel: 598 00 55
Open: daily, noon–11pm
Italian **AZN60**

Aristocrat is a typically Bakuvian example of the Old Azeri proverb 'more is most definitely more'. From the clear perspex baby grand piano to the solid-gold bathroom fittings and even – I kid you not – loo bowls, no expense has been spared air-freighting the very best of European uber-luxury to make your dining experience just a little more lavish. It's a little like an explosion in a Versace showroom. A mezzanine in the first room houses the VIP room where the owner – an 'important individual' – can lord it over the aristocratic rabble. Walls are hung with portraits of suitably haughty looking European aristo couples, while tables are bedecked in more gold, with top-grade imported tableware, as one would expect. The menu is Italian and very good – the black pasta being a particular favourite.

Food 9, Service 9, Atmosphere 8

Azza Fyujin *(right)*
Isr Plaza, 17th floor
Torgova
Tel: 498 24 02 www.azza.az
Open: daily, noon–11pm
Asian Fusion **AZN55**

Perched high, atop ISR Plaza, the Azza Fyujin (which is 'Asian' for fusion – geddit?) enjoys the same splendid night-time view across the glittering city to the TV Tower as the Azza Bar,

with which it shares the 17th floor. The menu here is a Chinese-leaning Asian fusion, with a smattering of Thai dishes and some reasonable, if not spectacular, sushi and other Japanese offerings. It is a sad fact, however, that as with any restaurant that is trying to be too many things to too many people, it fails to wholly impress at any one of them. That having been said, the food is more than adequate – the kung po prawn is particularly delicious – the service is friendly and efficient and the whole is a perfectly reasonable experience. Watch out for the Business Lunch, where the menu turns inexplicably European.

Food 7, Service 8, Atmosphere 9

Bah Bah *(bottom)*
Aliyarbekhov St, 9
Torgova
Tel: 498 87 34
www.bah-bahclub.com
Open: daily, 12.30–11pm
Azeri **AZN25**

'Bah-Bah' means 'good', or 'bravo!' in Azeri and, while perhaps not entirely modest, is a very apt description of this reliable local restaurant, attractively bedecked in Azeri traditional handicrafts. Always busy and with friendly, if sometimes a little over-earnest, service, Bah-Bah is a great place to sample Azeri cuisine for the uninitiated. A live band provides an appropriate musical backdrop of traditional folk music, sometimes breaking into less traditional Beatles' medleys over an electronically-generated bossanova beat, which does lend a certain tropical pool-side atmosphere. The food is also

good. *Dushbara* (mutton broth with small raviolini-like meat-filled pasta twists) is to die for and the *shüyüd plov* (herby rice) with *narbiç* (chicken stewed with ground walnuts and pomegranates) are also stand-out. If in a larger group, consider also a *saj* – meat and/or fish and potatoes served sizzling on a traditional wide skillet.

Food 8, Service 8, Atmosphere 8

....

Beyrut *(left)*
Taghiyev St, 19
Torgova
Tel: 598 06 65
Open: daily, 10am–2am
Lebanese   **AZN35**

The décor might not be up to much, but it's the Lebanese cuisine that has made Beyrut such a favourite with Azeris and foreigners in-the-know, to say nothing of Baku's fairly large expat Lebanese community. While the presentation of the restaurant may be nothing to write home about, the same certainly can't be said of the food. *Muttabal* (aubergine dip) comes studded with pomegranate seeds; houmous is a creamy whirl scattered with chopped parsley, while the *fattoush* salad has just the right balance of sharp, citrus tang and fresh, coarse-chopped garden herbs. On the main courses, the simply named 'rice with meat' is a great unctuous hunk of slow-baked mutton, which melts like butter in your mouth, served with a *plov* cooked to perfection and sprinkled with raisins, browned onions and toasted cashews. Makes my mouth water just thinking about it.

Food 9, Service 7, Atmosphere 7

Bibi *(right)*
Abdulla Shaig St, 241
Nasimi
Tel: 510 26 32
Open: daily, noon–midnight
Persian   **AZN20**

Behind a rather unprepossessing exterior, Bibi opens up like a fable in the 1001 Arabian Nights. Owner Reza decided after some years in Baku that what the city really needed was a decent Persian restaurant and Bibi is the fruit of all his labour. Pleasingly popular with Persian ex-pats, Bibi is a wonderful mix of East and West, with rush-matted ceilings, great chandeliers, kilims on walls and curious portraits of Europeans, in partly Asiatic dress. The meal starts with an enormous puffed up Persian *lavash*, or flatbread, shiny with butter and dotted with black poppy seeds. Many great Persian dishes share a common ancestor with Azeri cuisine, so be on the look-out for a Persian take on chicken with walnuts and pomegranate, best served with barberry rice. Be sure and stay for tea and hunks of delicious honeyed preserved quince after your meal too.

Food 9, Service 8, Atmosphere 8

....

Caravansera *(top)*
Gala (Qala) St, 11
Old City
Tel: 492 66 68
Open: daily, noon–3pm, 6.30–11pm
Azeri   **AZN25**

Entering Caravansera is like entering another era. A restaurant since 1973, the 14th century caravansera is a courtyard with a central water fountain

– where your camel would have been tethered back in the day – with 15 original, private dining rooms recessed into the walls around. Across the street is the overflow restaurant, which has a huge subterranean communal dining room, with the most amazing, vast beaten copper door on a central hinge upon which it pivots. Each of the private rooms is lined with wonderful ceramic tiles and glorious textiles and the tables laid with starched white linen. It is a shame, then, that the food and service nothing like match the absolute singularity of the atmosphere. Adequately prepared dishes have a tendency all to arrive at once, so it is as well to order in stages. Flaming torch-lit live music on a Sunday evening adds to the ambience.

Food 7, Service 7, Atmosphere 10

 Cio Cio San *(top)*
Badalbeyli St, 98
Torgova
Tel: 498-02-72
Open: daily, noon–1am
Japanese   **AZN50**

Named after the eponymous heroine of Puccini's Madame Butterfly, Cio Cio San is a very good high-end Japanese just around the corner from the Jazz Centre. Design is strong and the backlit *shoji*-style wall in particular lends an effective, 'faux-authentic' touch. Waiters memorise your order, which is all well and good if their memories are spot on, but occasional mishaps do occur. Indeed, the service aims high, but occasionally falls just short of its mark, a criticism that could be applied also to the food. The menu reads excitingly

and dishes are generally prepared to an extremely high standard, however some dishes are not quite there – a scallop, just a tad over-cooked, a few stray seeds or a smear of sauce on an otherwise cleanly presented dish – but these are tiny quibbles and a meal here is a perfectly enjoyable, if not enjoyably perfect, night out.

Food 9, Service 8, Atmosphere 9

Dalida Deluxe *(bottom)*
3rd Floor, Nargiz Mall,
Fountains Sq, Torgova
Tel: 496 88 61 www.dalida.az
Open: daily, noon–1am
International   **AZN45**

There is something about the cavernous hall at Dalida, with its huge domed ceiling, honey-coloured wood and dusky blue fabric which is a little like the swankiest restaurant on a giant cruise ship – you know, the one with the Captain's Table. Dalida Deluxe – not to be confused with the unremarkable Dalida Café across the way – is the fine dining half of the brand and the dining here is indeed fine. The menu is unashamedly international and the Italian dishes, especially, are tasty, well-prepared and presented with great panache. For this hedonist, however, it's dining al fresco on the terrace that really takes some beating. Sitting with a glass of wine and a bowl of gnocchi on a balmy summer's evening, looking over Fountain Square and across to the gloriously technicoloured flood-lighting of the TV Tower is pure magic.

Food 8, Service 7, Atmosphere 7

Finestra *(left)*
Nakchivani St, 14
Nasimi
Tel: 436 78 54
Open: daily, noon–11pm
Italian   **AZN45**

From the same management as Mado and Penjere, both of which also mean window in, respectively, Japanese and Azeri, Finestra is a good, solid Italian option that, while it perhaps lacks the convivial atmosphere of Scalini, or the upscale panache of Mosaico, certainly has more to offer than just a decent pizza. Popular with business folk at lunchtime and a younger crowd – who tend to congregate in the booths up on the mezzanine – later in the day, Finestra has a lengthy menu, featuring all the usual Italian suspects as well as some Azeri staples like sturgeon with pomegranate. Oh and don't be fooled by the Italian name badges on the waiters in their natty, if toggle-free, 'tricolore' boy-scout scarves, I'd put money on Fredo having been born Elchin.

Food 7, Service 7, Atmosphere 8

Firuza *(right)*
Tarlan Aliyarbeyov St, 14
Torgova
Tel: 318 65 45
Open: daily, 10am–1am
Azeri   **AZN20**

Descending the steps into Firuza, you could be forgiven for thinking you had entered some kind of Disney dungeon. Ok, the fibreglass rocks and beams do not exactly scream authenticity, but, when taken with the myriad plates, kilims and other more traditional hang-ings, it all comes together and even works, albeit in a sort of Caucasian chalet meets cellar kind of way. The food, however, is memorable in a far better way. *Lürma boğçada* is a sort of outsized pasty – stewed meat, apples and various dried fruit are placed in a bread-like pastry shell and baked to shiny perfection. Lip-smackingly good and seriously filling. Other, lighter dishes come off just as well. The menu is long and, to many westerners, all but impenetrable, but the smiling staff will be happy to help you decipher their wares.

Food 8, Service 7, Atmosphere 7

Georgian Home *(bottom)*
Mirza Ibrahimov St, 18
Torgova
Tel: 367 58 05
Open: daily, 6pm–11pm
Georgian   **AZN40**

Undoubtedly the most visually impressive of Baku's many Georgian restaurants, the interior of Georgian Home is somehow more Alice in Wonderland than anything you might expect from Tbilisi or elsewhere across the border. The combination of beautiful, pierced ceramics, hanging lamps, tables on angled platforms and reflective surfaces is breathtaking, but don't think for a moment that this is a tactic to divert you from any shortcomings in the food. From the first mouthful of cheese and garlic filled *khachapuri* bread – like an oozingly unctuous filled naan bread – you know you're onto a winner. In its six years the Georgian Home has chalked up a lot of loyal followers and an impressive amount of press

coverage, both here in Azerbaijan and back home in Georgia. It is easy to see why.

Food 8, Style 8, Atmosphere 9

 **The Grill** *(top)*
Hyatt Regency,
Bakikhanov St, 1, Nasimi
Tel: 496 12 34
www.baku.regency.hyatt.com
Open: daily, noon–3pm, 6.30–11pm
International　　　　　**AZN85**

Recently reopened after renovation by London-based Wilsdon Design Associates, who currently handle all Hyatt design globally, The Grill restaurant is visually stunning. WDA have made great use of the restaurant's original 30 foot pillars, wonderful cornices and ceiling roses and have come up with an almost edible design in shades of chocolate and cream that is at once warm and inviting and toweringly impressive. Service is top-notch and the menu, as befits the main restaurant in the Hyatt estate, is also a perfect example of what a high-end grill restaurant should offer – a pared down list of classic grill dishes, prepared to perfection. Beef is sourced from Nebraskan Black Angus herds, there is a good selection of seafood, all the right salads and sauces and a short, but carefully chosen list of New and Old World wines.

Food 9, Service 9, Atmosphere 9

Ibrus Wine Bar *(left)*
Mirza Mansur St, 73
Old City
Tel: 492 44 61

www.ibruswineclub.com
Open: daily, 11am–11pm
International　　　　　**AZN35**

A welcome new addition to the Old City scene, The Ibrus Wine Club, as its name suggests, is really more of a wine tasting outfit with a decent kitchen than a restaurant in the traditional sense. Off the street, you descend into a subterranean world of 14th century tunnels and cleverly excavated pits and wells, visible through glass floors. Currently serving a good, if small, selection of Azeri wines from the Shamakha, Shirvan and Ismailli regions, this list is currently bolstered by imported wines, sold at a premium, as Azeri tastes demand. The longer term plan, however, is to expand the native and organic lists and, ultimately, be all Azeri, when tastes permit. Good luck to them, we say, and with an interesting and well-executed international menu and Azeri dishes also available by prior arrangement, supporting Ibrus is really no hardship at all.

Food 7, Style 7, Atmosphere 9

Imereti *(right)*
Khagani St, 13
Torgova
Tel: 493 41 81
Open: daily, 6pm–midnight
Georgian　　　　　**AZN16**

Endlessly recommended as the place to come for traditional Georgian food and hospitality, Imereti can be a challenge to locate. Discreet, to put it mildly, the signage is at about knee level and the entrance down some steps below. Inside, the slightly overly bright dining

eat...

71

room is dotted with quaint pictures of Georgian scenes and dolls in national costume and the like – faintly kitsch, sure, but taken together, pleasingly nostalgic. Food is excellent, though the menu somewhat impenetrable to the uninitiated. But don't worry the staff speak some English and will be happy to help. We recommend *khinkhali* – large spiced ravioli – and *chashushuli* – a heavily spiced meat stew. The atmosphere is jolly and convivial, with families and groups of friends sharing jugs of very moreish *cha-cha* (Georgian grappa) with diners at their own – and other – tables.

Food 9, Service 8, Atmosphere 8

Jasmine *(left)*
Bridge Plaza, Bakhikhanov St, 6
AREA
Tel: 404 54 04
www.bic.az
Open: daily, noon–11pm
Chinese/Thai   **AZN45**

Jasmine (Chinese) and Siam (Thai) have now been absorbed into one restaurant, occupying one side of the third floor of Bridge Plaza, freeing up the other side for the so-so Mediterranean, Olive. With an attractive dining room, all chinese good luck scarlet, with fans, carved fretwork screens and other bits of chinoiserie and big revolving lazy susans on the 8-seater round tables, the atmosphere is spot on for a family-friendly, neighbourhood Chinese. The menu leans heavily to the Chinese side too and features some regional specialities like a great Szechuan hot and spicy soup. Its solid range of Thai staples impress as well though

and its no surprise to find that among its clientele of ex-pats are, crucially, a lot of the Chinese Embassy staff, who come in their droves on Sunday lunchtimes.

Food 7, Service 7, Atmosphere 7

Mado *(bottom)*
Inshaatchilar Ave, 33
Nasimi
Tel: 497 55 44
Open: daily, noon–11pm
Japanese   **AZN50**

Yet another reliable Japanese, Mado is sister restaurant to Penjere (see page 81) and Finestra (see page 70) and has spent the past two and a half years carving out a niche and solid reputation among the business crowds and ex-pats of the Nasimi area. Indeed, it is always a good sign to see the odd Japanese face among the ex-pat regulars and that is testament to the Filipino-born, Japanese-trained chef's evident skill. The menu offers a good selection of all the usual fare and, less usual, including ostrich teppanyaki, which I think one can confidently assume is not available anywhere else in Baku or, indeed, elsewhere in the Caucasus. The interior is pleasantly decorated, if perhaps a little sparse, and the service warm, welcoming and friendly. One stand-out dish on the reliable menu has to be the *gyoza* – extremely tasty and worryingly moreish!

Food 9, Service 8, Atmosphere 8

Mesa Lounge *(right)*
Hajibeyov St, 38/3

Torgova
Tel: 598 88 66
www.mesalounge.az
Open: daily, 5pm–midnight
Japanese/European   **AZN60**

Looking incongruously like some medieval castle fantasy from the street, Mesa Lounge really surprises with its interior. The restaurant on the top floor would do any Spaniard proud – swathes of red and gold chiffon are draped from a vaulted ceiling over plate-glass windows that open in the summer for an almost al fresco experience. Potted palms and banana plants complete the Spanish harem effect and teams of helpful staff buzz around waiting on the highly fashionable mainly 20- and 30-something crowd. Japanese and European menus both excel, especially the unusual crunchy hot *maki* rolls from the former and the rib-eye with foie gras from the latter. After dinner, try one of the handmade fruit *kalyan* – a *shisha* drawn through a hollowed piece of fruit for a surprisingly intense flavour hit. For more on the excellent first floor bar (see Drink).

Food 9, Service 9, Atmosphere 9

 Mosaico   *(top)*
Alizadeh St, 14
Torgova
Tel: 493 61 93
Open: daily, noon–midnight
Italian   **AZN65**

A shimmering vision in shades of slate and gunmetal, with glittering crystal bead curtains, black leather furniture and indulgent, attentive service to match, it is no surprise that Mosaico

has become the premier upscale Italian restaurant in Baku. The crowd is visibly wealthy – think half a Milan catwalk of top-notch design labels and shades perched ostentatiously atop expensively coiffed hair – and that's just the men. One of the more expensive tables in town, food here is beautifully prepared and presented representing a broad selection of Italian regional cuisine, with a special emphasis on seafood and fresh, home-made pasta. As one would expect, mozzarella is buffalo; *salumeria* all imported from Italy and the coffee is, unusually for Baku, excellent. Upstairs is an all white VIP room and dining suite, that seats sixteen straight out of a Jay-Z video.

Food 8, Service 9, Atmosphere 9

 Mugham Club   *(bottom)*
Rzayeva St, 9
Old City
Tel: 492 40 85
Open: daily, 5pm–midnight
Azeri   **AZN50**

Surely one of the world's most atmospheric restaurants, The Mugham Club is situated in an unusual two-storey caravansera, more on which can be found in its listing in Culture. The central courtyard is open to the stars (with a cover in bad weather) and dominated by two large fig trees, bedecked in fairy lights. Fascinating photos of yesteryear Baku adorn stone walls of recessed nooks, etched with ancient Arabic graffiti. All tables angle towards the stage, where impressive displays of traditional dance and *mugham* song go on throughout the evening. Food is good, service attentive and it is no

eat...

surprise that this is perhaps Baku's premier tourist restaurant. Do bargain hard if buying beautiful handicrafts from shops lining the upper gallery though – this ain't a tourist trap for nothing.

Food 8, Service 9, Atmosphere 10

 Occo *(left)*
Hajibeyov St, 51
Torgova
Tel: 493 88 00 www.occo.az
Open: daily, 5pm–1am
European   **AZN60**

Occo's motto 'the art of fine dining' sets the bar high and over the past couple of years or so, it has continued to perform for its well-heeled, mainly 30 something clientele. From the back-lit golden agate bar, like a giant slab of luminescent honeycomb, to the re-curring 'o' theme in the recessed wall lights, wall-mounted wine rack and delicate pendant glass bubble lamps, you know that a lot of thought has gone into 'the look'. Great news is that the food lives up to the design's promise too. Signature Hennessy house cocktails are served short in a tumbler, the 'Occo' being poured over a squeeze of freshly pounded strawberry puree and garnished with mint – an intensity of flavour that explodes in the mouth. Food is exquisite, service good and the attention to detail impressive to say the least.

Food 9, Service 9, Atmosphere 9

 Old City *(right)*
Mammadov St, 24

Old City
Tel: 492 05 55
Open: daily, 1pm–11pm
Azeri   **AZN45**

Somehow the hardboard cut-out of a jolly fat chef by the steps down to the popular Old City (Köhna Shahar) res-taurant implies a certain 'Little Chef' quality, which couldn't do the work of multi-award winning chef Shahhus-sein Kerimov a greater injustice. The two dining rooms are pleasantly kitted out in kilims and pieces of traditional Azeri art and crafts, the light perhaps a little over-bright, but the atmosphere works. It's when the food comes out, however, that your juices really start to flow. *Lavangi* are little bite-sized rolls of sturgeon or chicken filled with a paste of walnuts and cherry plums, the *plovs* (pilaf) are to die for. There really is nothing on the menu that doesn't sing and, with friendly waiters eager to practice their variable English, you'll manage to make the best of a difficult to penetrate menu.

Food 10, Service 9, Atmosphere 8

 Paul's *(bottom)*
Zagarpala St/Rafibayli St
Torgova
Tel: 050 502 55 07
Open: 6–11pm. Closed Sundays.
German/Swiss   **AZN30**

In a desert city of surprising and id-iosyncratic places, Paul's Swiss/Ger-man chalet restaurant and beer garden must take the teutonic biscuit. Deserv-edly famed for their delicious steak – sourced from Brazil, marinated to a special recipe and cooked to perfec-

tion on an outside grill, Paul's also does a fine line in *spëtzle*, *schnitzels*, sausages, fondues and, in winter, a deliciously spiced *glüwein*. In summer, a mainly ex-pat crowd fills the astonishingly green 100 odd seater beer garden – the garden was the work of a former Baku resident ex-pat from Greece – while in winter, a marginally smaller sub-section of the same crowd crams into the cosy, wolf-skin-lined chalet-style restaurant itself for some good old alpine cheer. A mainstay of the foreign crowd in Baku, Paul's is also the place to come to source reliable quality caviar to take home.

Food 8, Service 8, Atmosphere 8

 Penjere *(top)*
Abdulla Shaig St, 245
Nasimi
Tel: 510-37-00
Open: daily, noon–11pm
Azeri **AZN35**

The first in the 'window' group of restaurants (Mado, Finestra) serves up top-notch Azeri cuisine in a a pleasingly eccentric environment. Immensely popular with a mainly Azeri crowd of suits, civvies and even the odd uniform, there is something almost alpine in feel about the al fresco dining garden and its few private dining rooms, a theme which is repeated in the wood-panelled main dining hall upstairs. The food here is excellent – as at Mado, ostrich features on the menu, but it's the more traditional fare that is the big draw here. Presentation is beautiful, with dustings of *sumaq*, scatterings of pomegranate and artfully folded cones

of *lavash* bread, but, as it should be, it's in the tasting that this pudding is proven. For the uninitiated, try the *gurza* – a little like an Azeri bite-sized *samosa* – lip-smackingly good.

Food 9, Style 8, Atmosphere 9

 Scalini *(bottom)*
Bakikhanov St, 2
Nasimi
Tel: 598 28 50
Open: daily, noon–2.30pm, 7pm–11pm
(noon–10.30pm Sun)
Italian **AZN55**

Ask any Bakuvian to name their favourite restaurants in town and there's a good chance you'll hear the name Scalini mentioned in the top three and it's easy to see why. Always busy, with a relaxed, convivial atmosphere and friendly staff, Scalini does exactly what you want from a homely Italian restaurant. With décor mixing classic film posters with chianti flasks and lit in the main by candles, it's no surprise then that this is where Pierce Brosnan dined when filming The World is Not Enough; nor that what's good enough for Bond should be good enough also for Jose Carreras. Chef/manager Elio Bevilacqua is originally from Calabria and learned his trade by the sea, so seafood is a particular focus, but in truth, the menu dots pleasingly around Italy and features regional specialities from pretty much everywhere, including great pizza.

Food 8, Service 9, Atmosphere 9

Shilla _(top)_
Khatai Ave, 51
Khatai
Tel: 417 01 02
Open: daily, 6–11pm
Korean fusion   **AZN45**

All new Shilla is Baku's first and only Korean restaurant. Located in a large, purpose built sandstone pagoda, the original plan was for an exclusively Korean menu. However, as Bakuvian tastes are not always so adventurous, it was decided to include some Thai and Japanese dishes too, to guide the diner in. All the food is good and innovative – the sandwich _maki_ from the sushi list being a case in point – but it is in the Korean food that the Thai chef, who cut his teeth at a Korean place in Bangkok, really excels. The _kimchi_ are intensely spicy, sweet, savoury and sour; the _pajeon_ pancake, meltingly tasty; while, come the main course, it is hard to look past the Korean barbecue – choice cuts of meat and veg to griddle at your table under a steel extractor hood, that marries perfectly with the restaurant's clean-lined design.

Food 8, Service 8, Atmosphere 8

Sultans _(middle)_
Khagani St, 10
Torgova
Tel: 598 05 55   www.sultans.az
Open: daily, 10am–midnight
Azeri   **AZN30**

A Baku institution, Sultan's motto is 'come hungry, we will fill your belly'. Entering the broad, carpeted hallway, you are greeted by a bustling throng of waiters and led through to the main hall, ceiling draped in billowing red fabric and lit by beautiful glass pendant lamps and coloured spots. Dominated by a long, open-plan kitchen and grill, the friendly, informal restaurant is filled with a mouth-watering barbecue smell. In summer the back opens up into the garden for alfresco dining, sadly something of a rarity in Baku these days. The menu runs the gamut of Azeri cuisine and is good throughout, but it's the kebabs that rule the day – especially the metre long Adana kebab, that serves 10 people for a very reasonable AZN70. Do specify downstairs when booking though, as harsh lighting upstairs destroys the convivial atmosphere.

Food 8, Service 8, Atmosphere 7

Terrace Garden _(bottom)_
Sultan Inn, Boyuk Gala St, 20
Old City
Tel: 437 23 05   www.sultaninn.com
Open: daily, 7am–1am
International   **AZN55**

At the Sultan Inn they like to do things differently and, as per the hotel and almost uniquely in Baku, small here is rightly considered beautiful. The intimate, conservatory dining room seats just 24 around an unusual central fireplace, housed in a glass pyramid, which not only provides a lovely focal point but adds a welcome cosiness and warmth. The European food is good, if not exceptional, and the service friendly and attentive. It is no surprise to find that the restaurant is often booked out. Clientele include hotel guests, sure, but also groups of well-heeled and

extremely well-dressed Bakuvians of all ages. Surrounded on three sides by a broad terrace, in summer you can also dine outside with wonderful views over the Maiden Tower, just a few metres away, and the Caspian Sea beyond.

Food 7, Service 9, Atmosphere 9

 Trattoria L'Oliva *(left)*
Taghiyev St, 14
Torgova
Tel: 493 09 54
www.trattoria-oliva.com
Open: daily, noon–midnight
Italian AZN50

In a great location for Torgova and the downtown area, L'Oliva is a very good, casual, alternative Italian to the more upscale and pricier Mosaico around the corner. The recently renovated restaurant is all Tuscan burnt pinks and umbers, with olive green woodwork and a pitch perfect selection of framed prints, potted olive plants and other Italophile decorative touches you'd expect in any restaurant of its

ilk. The menu features the usual classic staples from all over Italy, done well and accompanied by an impressive and well-priced (for Baku) wine list. Ever-popular with a loyal crowd of foreigners and locals alike, after a delicious dinner you can pop downstairs to the Red Olive Lounge (see Drink) and sink into a deep leather armchair for a brandy or two.

Food 8, Service 9, Atmosphere 8

 (Xasar) Khazar *(middle)*
Underneath Bibi Heybat
 Mosque, Sabayil District
Tel: 050 584 88 84
Open: daily, 9am–11pm
Azeri fish AZN20

Universally known to those in the know just as 'that great fish place by the mosque' Khazar is one of Baku's best-kept dining secrets. Located in the Sabayil region and with no real address, Khazar is situated right on the rather unprepossessing seafront at the very end of a tiny road, just beyond the

majestic new Bibi Heybat Mosque. It does indeed also serve the best fish in Baku and at an extremely good price too. For a flat rate of AZN 20, teams of happy, smiling young waiters – few of whom speak Russian, let alone English but who are fluent in 'point and smile' – will bring you trays of small dishes of mezze (you just point and choose the ones you fancy), followed by a huge Caspian sea-fish, fried to perfection and served with mountains of salad and rice or chips.

Food 9, Service 8, Atmosphere 7

 Zakura *(right)*
Alizadeh St, 9
Torgova
Tel: 498 18 18   www.zakura.az
Open: daily, noon–3pm, 6pm–2am
Japanese   **AZN65**

Designed by London-based firm Blue Sky Hospitality, Zakura brings a world-class edge to Baku's dining scene. Based around the Isikaya bar concept - small, tapas-style dishes – Zakura seeks to give a Bakuvian twist to its food. Slatted shades cast sculptural shadows across silver calligraphy on grey walls with accents of red and gold lacquer. Food is designed by executive chef Kenneth Lim, ex of Nobu London, who brings an appreciable Nobu accent to the menu – the black cod with miso takes you straight back to Park Lane. Excellent sashimi is ever-so-lightly seared and marinated in sesame and soy. Sushi rice is seasoned perfectly, rolls melt in your mouth and the *nigiri* come topped with the likes of flakes of gold leaf to add a touch of opulence. The Sunday all you can eat buffet for AZN 30 is especially good value.

Food 9, Service 9, Location 9

drink...

A little caveat before we commence – the Baku drinking scene is not the most evolved on the planet. Although there are plenty of pleasant options to wile away an evening, this is no New York or London and, as with any developing scene, things change fast. It must be remembered that, although the sale and consumption of alcohol is legal and, more importantly, widely tolerated, this is a Muslim country and the culture of drinking and bar-hopping that many Westerners may be used to simply does not exist here. By the same token, the party scene is often not clearly delineated either and most of the venues listed in Party have made that cut by dint of being, sometimes only marginally, more high-octane or having a greater emphasis on live music, dance floor, karaoke or some element of spectacle. It is certainly worth browsing both sections for a full and broad cross-section of what Baku has to offer after the sun goes down.

In terms of bars proper that serve decent cocktails, these do tend to centre around the hotel scene – The Landmark's Sky Bar; Park Inn's Mirvari; The Radisson Blu's Azza, Sultan Inn's Q Bar and Excelsior's L'Atelier to name a few. These are really the gold standard for stylish drinking in Baku. Outside of the hotels all is certainly not a barren wasteland, however, and an increasing number of interesting independent establishments have cropped up over the past decade or so. The recent boom in the oil industry and its attendant influx of oil money has led to a growing class of young people with some disposable income and they are increasingly well-served. Notable in this category are Mesa near Government House, The Living Rooms off Fountain Square, Kishmish and Kill Bill in the Old City and both The Lounge and Opera Lounge (see Party) near the Hyatt. Brand new

openings Chinar and The World Fashion Lounge (for both see Party) look likely to be welcome new additions to that list too.

The majority of watering holes on the street, however, centre around Fountain Square and are of the identikit ex-pat pub variety, which, for the most part, have questionable lighting and variable atmosphere. Most have a pool table, many also a darts board, or other pub entertainment. Many also come with half-cut ladies of dubious virtue, who may or may not be available for a price. We have included the best of these pubs which, by quirk of atmosphere, décor, service, management style, kitchen or some other feature have set themselves up a cut above the rest.

Come summertime and Baku is cowed by stifling heat and, up to a few years back at least, decamps to an outdoor 'terrace' establishment. Sadly, a rather ill-conceived, city-wide clean up nearly a decade ago closed down many of these establishments. Some that remain, however, are the Hayat *Çay Evi* or Tea House (see Snack) by the Russian Embassy, which, despite being nominally a tea house, has beer taps prominent, and the excellent Paul's (see Eat) which has a beer garden seating around 120 in a green and pleasant courtyard setting. For the younger at heart, Metkarting (see Play,) has a go-kart track and plunge pool to throw into the mix with its beer garden too. As we go to press, Molokan Gardens, once home to the much-missed pond-side Fisherman's Wharf, and Fountain Square are still behind boards being reconstructed. One can only hope that their new designs will also include somewhere to enjoy a drink in the great outdoors.

Adam's Sports *(left)*
Abdulkarim Ali-Zadeh St, 6
Torgova
Tel: 498 12 89
Open: daily, noon–2am

Known as 'the Cheers of Baku', as it is where everyone knows your name, Adam's has been serving the ex-pat population with a smile, in various guises and from various locations, for 11 years now, making it among the oldest ex-pat pubs in Baku. Originally run as an American diner and with a US diner menu to match, Brit regulars questioned why the Indian-born owners weren't serving curry. They thought about this, imported a restaurant team from their native Mumbai and so one of the best pubs in Baku became also one of the best curry houses in Baku. With a winner-stays on pool policy, all major sporting events screened on large screens and a friendly clientele of locals and ex-pats, Adam's is also one of the easiest places in Baku to win friends, if perhaps not influence people.

ALZ Club *(right)*
Rashid Behbudov St, 8
Torgova
Tel: 498 01 04
Open: daily, 1pm–2am

Discreetly signed and lying in a basement under the more visible Café City (see Snack), the ALZ Club has been serving up cocktails and *kalyans* (shisha pipes) for a couple of years now. The padded leather wall panels, mood lighting, deep velvet sofas and glass-topped tables with leather coasters give it a bit of a Caucasian gentleman's club feel, while the backlit city skylines over the windows lend a sophisticated edge – as well as, Vegas-like, making it impossible to note much in the way of the passage of time. The cocktails are good here, but it is manager Eldar's *kalyans* fashioned out of outsized vegetables that are the real draw. Open til late, ALZ attracts a mixed crowd from twenty-somethings through to the odd stray suit, and is a great place to come for a quiet drink – or smoke – away from the madding crowd.

Arabesque *(bottom)*
Yusif Mammadaliyev St, 19
Torgova
Tel: 580 00 00
www.arabesque.az
Open: daily, noon–3am

From the stuffed camel at the foot of the stairs to the fabulous chandelier glittering over the shimmering, many-textured golden walls of the atrium, you know that thought has gone into Arabesque from the get-go. Seating is at booths, with a low light emanating from behind carved fretwork screens – so far so upscale Arab. The banquette seats are upholstered in gorgeous Azeri textiles and kilims, which offer a nice counterpoint to the stained glass pendant lamp mood lighting. The service is attentive and the drinks list is good. Particularly popular with the hip young things of Baku's nocturnal scene, Arabesque is a great place to swing by and kick back over a few drinks or, indeed, sample the pan-arab and pizza snack menu. Afterwards you can climb the stairs to the cushion-lined shisha room, lay out and chill with a fruity concoction from the extensive *kalyan* list.

drink...

Azza Bar   (top)
ISR Plaza 17th Floor
Torgova
Tel: 598 11 33 www.azza.az
Open: daily, 4pm–2am

Low-level lighting over leather sofas and wingback chairs and a good list of reasonably priced and, crucially, beautifully executed cocktails are just a few reasons to love the Azza Bar in ISR Plaza. Another, of course, is the incredible view over the rooftops around Fountain Square and across the glittering city to the one and only TV tower up on the hill beyond. With live jazz on Wednesday, Friday and Saturday evenings and a soul, jazz, funk CD soundtrack at other times, it is no wonder that this has become the watering hole of choice for many Baku residents and regular visitors, as well as the more expected guests at the Radisson, with whom it shares the 17th floor of ISR Plaza. A pared down menu of salads, sandwiches, burgers and sushi from the next door Azza Fyujin restaurant (see Eat) is also on offer.

Beluga Bar   (middle)
Hyatt Regency, Bakikhanov St, 1
Nasimi
Tel: 490 12 34
www.baku.regency.hyatt.com
Open: daily, 5pm–2am

You can often gauge a hotel bar by the number of non-residents who drink there and, judging by the popularity of this one, something is obviously being done right. With a list of some 16 vodkas served at room temperature or frozen, the Hyatt Regency's Beluga Bar is deservedly the number one

stop for aficionados of what the Russians named 'little water'. Like the rest of the Hyatt Regency, the Beluga Bar has recently seen a refit, courtesy of London-based designers WDA, and is now looking as refreshingly cool as a frozen bottle of its signature drink. As per the wine list in the next-door Grill restaurant, the cocktail list is short and carefully thought out. Their chocolate martini is vodka-based, of course, and sinfully tasty. At the other end of the taste scale, they also mix a mean Bloody Mary.

Brewery Pub   (bottom)
Istiglaliyyat St, 27
Old City
Tel: 437 28 68
www.bakubrewery.com
Open: daily, 11am–midnight

A German-style microbrewery with three styles of excellent homemade beer is not, perhaps, what one might expect to turn up in your average desert city. But then Baku is no average desert city. The beer-making equipment was imported, along with recipes and all the key ingredients, straight from the fatherland and is now housed upstairs in a spotless controlled environment – the old-school copper apparatus on display down below being for decorative purposes only. Plans are afoot for a bottling plant, which will be housed elsewhere, due to noise complaints from neighbours, but for now, Salm Brau, as the light, medium and dark brews are collectively known, is available only here. Bavarian waitress uniforms, the carved pine-clad room, with it's German country kitchen-style snug out back and the delicious sausages on

drink...

the excellent bar menu all compliment the teutonic theme nicely.

Corner Bar *(top)*
Corner of Tolstoy St & Rasul Rza St, Torgova
Tel: 494 89 55
www.thecornerbaku.com
Open: daily, 6pm–4am

More than just another ex-pat dive, The Corner bar has established itself as a mainstay of the Baku entertainment scene. With live music – rock, rock and more rock – on Thursday, Friday and Saturday nights, this has left the management with a Sunday slot to fill with, er, rock. Sundays in fact are given over to up-and-coming bands and niche forms of rock, like metal, in its various forms. The bar has also played host to art exhibitions, featuring up and coming artists both local and international, and a quick look at the hundreds of old posters plastered over the entrance gives some idea of how much The Corner has contributed over the years. Popular with a youngish crowd of students, ex-pats and rockers of all ages, The Corner is definitely a place to be seen, if not heard.

Finnegans *(left)*
Abdulkarim Ali-zadeh St, 8
Torgova
Tel: 498 65 64
Open: daily, 11am–2am

Baku's premier Irish pub, Finnegans is, as you'd hope and expect, one of the few places in town to serve up a decent pint of the black stuff. Always busy, it gets rammed on Wednesdays and Saturdays, when a live band plays a folksy rock and Country and Western set to a wildly enthusiastic audience. The clientele is a friendly mix of ex-pat and local, who all seem to enjoy the craic. Food is standard pub grub, but does feature perhaps the city's only (and certainly a very decent) pie and mash as well as an all day breakfast, with – shock, horror – HP sauce (complete with Arabic branding and ingredient list). The pleasant setting is much like any other emerald isle themed pub in the world, with plenty of pub kitsch, proverbs on plaques about Paddy's fondness of the bottle and so on.

Kill Bill *(right)*
Hagigat Rzayeva St, 7
Old City
Tel: 497 13 77
Open: daily, noon–11pm

Now three years old, this homage to Tarantino's film of the same name moved around the corner to its current location in late 2008 to make way for the inevitable Bakuvian progress of construction at its old site. As one might expect from a bar called Kill Bill, the décor features some Japanese touches – like faux *shoji* screens - as well as framed stills and posters from the movie. Very effective use is made of the site's original vaulted ceilings, hung with different sized large balloon lamps. The crowd is bohemian, studenty and kind of off-beat cool and the mood lighting and comfy lounge seating, together with a discreet location that's just off the beaten Old City track, make this a great place to come

for a clandestine rendezvous for cocktails and maybe some of their pretty decent sushi.

Kishmish *(top)*
Kichik Gala St, 108
Old City
Tel: 492 91 82 www.kishmish.az
Open: daily, 2pm–midnight

Kishmish – meaning raisin – is a funny and rather wonderful old place. With a menu featuring 150 different teas, served with a variety of sweets that includes all the usual Middle Eastern classics, only more so – dates and figs are listed by country of origin, as are no less than three different colours of raisin. The cocktail list is equally lengthy and, among the 150 on the menu, includes such gems as the Queen Elizabeth – a mysterious concoction in festive red and green that combines being both very strong and very bitter. Far more palatable are the hot coffee cocktails, rum grog and various fruit sours. The decor is pleasingly eccentric and includes a row of cabinets of curiosities that each reflects a different city around the world. London contains miniature double deckers, post boxes and old-style phone booths, as well it should.

Konti *(left)*
Nizami St, 17
Torgova
Tel: 498 91 91
Open: daily, 1pm–12.30am

Just a hop, skip and a short jump from the Landmark building, British Embassy and Government House, it is no surprise that Konti is the watering hole of choice for many a suited or diplomatic type, sometimes even with scary looking suited entourage in tow. Lined with split wood panelling and furnished in a rather theme-parkish Wild West style the bar is filled with heavy, rough-cut chairs and tables. The Davey Crockett look is further developed by wall-mounted bear and raccoon skins, flintlock guns and antler lamps and so on. But the real draw at Konti is the self-service beer. Each table sits beneath a huge (fake) beer barrel, with a tap and a counter. You simply pour yourself a pint – or a litre – and the counter adds it to your tab. A nice gimmick and one which certainly seems to draw the crowds.

L'Atelier *(right)*
Excelsior, Heydar Aliyev Pr, 2
Khatai
Tel: 496 80 00
www.excelsiorhotelbaku.az
Open: daily, 5pm–4am

From the wall of Impressionist-inspired art, to the deco-with-a-twist chandeliers, via the fresh cut flowers and asymmetric, plush velvet banquette seating in soft shades of mauve, L'Atelier oozes all the opulent, luxuriant style and sophistication you'd expect from the bar at the opulent, luxurious and sophisticated Excelsior Hotel. Expert staff mix a mean cocktail here, or, if mixed drinks are not your thing, just sink into one of those oh-so-comfy chairs and sip on a large scotch on the rocks from a good, solid, heavy-bottomed tumbler. Realistically, it is a little

drink...

off the beaten track for most non-residents, but for hotel guests and anyone who finds themselves in the area, it is a great place – and far away from the crowds – to enjoy a quiet, relaxing nightcap or three at the end of a long, hard day.

 Living Room 1 *(left)*
Z. Taghiyev St, 17
Torgova
Tel: 493 87 25
www.livingroom.az
Open: daily, 11pm–6am

All scarlet walls and velvet curtains, gauzy drapes and silky plush sofas, with cutesy little tasselled bolster cushions, that once you've sunk into, you'll struggle to escape, there's something about Living Room 1 (and, indeed its sister establishment Living Room 2 (see Party) that feels more than a little boudoirish. With a pool table out back, a regular Russian language Mafia game (see Play) and a cheap menu of Indian fusion snacks and light bites served up til late, there's something on offer for pretty much everyone. Ultra-friendly, the twenty- and thirty-something creative crowd is mixed and, unusually for Baku, very gay-friendly. This is one living room where you're as likely to rub shoulders with a chart-topping pop star as the Dean of Admissions at Baku University.

 The Lounge *(right)*
Bakikhanov St, 2
Nasimi
Open: 7pm–1am (2am Fri/Sat).
Closed Sundays.

There is something about The Lounge's marble floor with slightly frayed carpets, the highly polished dark wood tables at booth seats with slightly worn upholstery, which lends just the right touch of faded grandeur to this unpretentious watering hole situated conveniently just across the road from the Hyatt. Under the same management as next door's Scalini (see Eat), The Lounge has a fiercely loyal crowd of regulars who pop in for a nightcap – and maybe a Havana – almost every night they are in town. Walls are bedecked in gold-framed portraits of Europeans in the wonderful garb of the nineteenth century 'Westerner gone native'. Curtains are long, red and velvet and nineteenth century Parisian scenes and 1930s ad posters complete the Paris-meets-Caucasus vibe. A great place to wile away an evening.

 Mesa Lounge *(top)*
Uzeyir Hajibeyov St, 38/3
Torgova
Tel: 598 88 66
www.mesalounge.az
Open: daily, 5pm–midnight

A perfect balance of Western gentleman's club and all the Eastern promise a man – or woman – could hope for. In design terms, Mesa's first floor bar is exactly what you would look to find in a city that marks the crossroads between Europe and Asia. Chocolate leather scroll top chairs are nicely set off by curtains of perforated hanging brass. In turn, the swirling, golden motif of the curtains is echoed on the dark wood panels of the saloon and again on the outsized lampshades, lined in chocolate silk. The crowd is a

suitably well-heeled mix of the super-wealthy and the super-slim, dressed to the nines in European labels and lured in by the impressive cocktails and sushi menu – complete with calorific values to help the super-wealthy stay super-slim – that is available from the upstairs restaurant.

Mirvari (top)
Park Inn, Azadlig Pr, 1
Torgova
Tel: 490 60 00
www.baku.rezidorparkinn.com
Open: daily, noon–3pm, 4pm–1am

In a city of astonishing night-time views, Mirvari's might just win by a short nose. Situated on the top floor of the so-so Park Inn Hotel, Mirvari is a tranquil haven of good design, chilled out lounge music, delicious cocktails and an excellent sushi menu. In summer you can take your drink out on to the terrace, with it's kitschy Haring-esque nightlights, and gaze down across the twinkling lights of Baku by night, reflected in the still waters of the Caspian. As we go to press, there is talk of making evening access to Mirvari available only to hotel guests and members, who will have to stump up a hefty annual membership fee, we can only hope they reconsider, but it might be worth your while calling the hotel ahead to guarantee entry into this sparkling gem of a bar.

Old Forester (middle)
Bashir Safar-oghlu St, 23
Torgova
Tel: 050 250 09 96
Open: daily, 10pm–2am

Now 18 months old, The Old Forester is a great, sprawling behemoth of an English-style pub, complete with faux Victorian etched mirrors around its booth seating, dark wood high bar stools and tables, surrounded by walls adorned with prints of the hunt, horse brasses and other pieces of classic pub paraphernalia. There is live jazz nightly, friendly and efficient staff, a long menu of international pub grub standards and all major sporting events are screened on giant, wall-mounted flatscreens. There is even an open fire with leather armchairs to sit and while away an afternoon with the papers over a pint or two or one of the 32 bottled beers. Popular with a predominantly thirty plus crowd of ex-pats and locals, the mezzanine level can also be booked out free of charge and is an ideal location for an informal private party.

Q Bar (bottom)
Sultan Inn, Boyuk Gala St, 20
Old City
Tel: 437 23 05
www.sultaninn.com
Open: daily, 6pm–2am

Perched atop the Sultan Inn (see Sleep) and sharing space the Terrace Garden restaurant (see Eat), the al fresco Q Bar is a smallish octagonal deck with a central bar and the same magnificent view across the main Old City Square to the Maiden Tower and the Caspian beyond. Instantly recognisable by its signature glowing fiery red lamps, visible from the Boulevard, the Q bar is a great place for an aperitif or, on sultry summers' nights, to spend an evening in a relaxed and oh-so-chilled vibe,

drink...

staying on into the wee small hours and hanging out for that refreshing hint of a night-time breeze. Soundtrack is lounge, the clientele for the most part dripping in designer labels – with the odd suited hotel guest – and you'll soon find that one of their excellent cocktails leads inexorably to another, and another and another.

Red Olive *(left)*
Zeynalabdin Taghiyev St, 14, Torgova
Tel: 493 09 54
www.trattoria-oliva.com
Open: daily, 6pm–5am

All ivory arches and deep red walls, hung with large gilt mirrors and outsized chandeliers; and plush velvet sofas that will grip you like a plush velvet vice, the Red Olive is also dotted with classically elegant standard and table lamps – both set to a pleasingly soporific dim – on polished dark wood side-tables. There's something about the Red Olive Lounge that feels a little like a Parisian salon, albeit one with a pronounced Caucasian twist. Cocktails are good, lighting is low, soundtrack is hip chill out and the crowd a pleasantly varied, mixed bunch of regulars – cool cats and suited types, both from Baku and beyond. So grab yourself a large one on the rocks in a chunky tumbler and perhaps even a post-prandial Havana, sink into an armchair and kick back a while – you, like the rest of this crowd, are not going anywhere.

Shakespeare *(middle)*
Abdulkarim Ali-zadeh St, 6
Torgova
Tel: 498 91 21
Open: daily, 11pm–4am

Another old-timer on the ex-pat pub scene, the Shakespeare has been at its present location for only a year or so, after moving from its former, decade-

long residency in Molokan Gardens, due to a rent increase. Always busy, with a friendly and very international crowd of ex-pats and Azeris vying to get on the winner-stays-on pool table. Live music – usually rock – on Fridays and Saturdays is also a big draw and weekend nights can be absolutely rammed. The staff are super-friendly, beer flows way into the wee small hours and the menu of club sandwiches and pub classics is far better than the so-so curry upstairs (for a spice fix, you're best off going next door to Adam's incidentally). Most surprisingly, perhaps, is the news that they have now opened a sister Shakespeare pub in Pattaya, Thailand, a sort of beach bard, one would imagine.

The Shark is a rare exception to the generally quite reliable unwritten local rule that one should never descend steps in Baku in search of a drink. It is also a welcome addition to the Hg2 short list of ex-pat pubs that are worth a visit. The managers – one Azeri, one British – have done a great job here and the friendly atmosphere pulls in a regular crowd of Azeris and (mainly British) ex-pats alike. As usual, there is a pool table and a menu of the usual, well-priced pub grub fare, as well as a happy hour, live sports on large screens and a decent weekend fry-up. What this place has that others may lack, however, is atmosphere, whether by dint of the better-than-average décor or a more than usually personal touch from the staff, the Shark has got something going on.

Shark *(right)*
Khagani St, 4
Torgova
Tel: 493 69 96
Open: daily, noon–2am

Sky Bar *(top)*
Landmark, Nizami St, 90
Torgova
Tel: 465 20 10
www.thelandmarkhotel.az
Open: daily, 9pm–2am

Surprisingly unknown, The Landmark Hotel's 17th Floor Sky Bar is one of Baku's best kept secrets, as well as being, in the words of their website, the 'soul' of the hotel. Spectacular views across the city are best enjoyed at night – as are the expertly mixed cocktails – to the accompaniment of their nightly live piano and jazz music. Unsurprisingly, the crowd is largely suited, but the atmosphere is warm and friendly and this is far more than just another businessman's bar. The Italian-designed sofas in shades of creams, beiges and taupes, with the odd burnt orange cushion as highlight, are as comfortable as they are achingly hip and contrast beautifully with the stripped bare concrete surround. Solitary stems in vases only enhance the minimalist uber-cool vibe in this, one of Baku's leading drinking spots.

Tortuga Pirate Bar *(left)*
Tarlan Aliyarbeyov St, 9
Torgova
Open: daily, noon–2am (5am Sat/Sun)

Baku's premier pirate-themed pub is, well, in actuality Baku's only pirate-themed pub. Named after the pirates' island in the Pirates of the Caribbean movie, this relative new-comer to the Baku ex-pat pub scene is a vision of pirate kitsch, complete with hand-painted mural replicas of the movie poster, walls bedecked in fishing nets filled with ships' wheels, treasure maps and more skulls and crossbones than you can shake a stick at. The young, friendly and dynamic Azeri management run a bunch of events and specials throughout the week for their mixed Azeri and ex-pat crowd, including a daily happy hour, good food, pool competitions, live sports on big screens and much more besides. And, as if that's not enough, most of the skull and crossboned chooch is on sale too. An appropriate souvenir of the Caucasus if ever there was one!

Vogue Café *(right)*
Tarlan Aliyarbeyov St, 6
Torgova
Tel: 498 75 03
Open: daily, 6pm–2am

As you'd expect from a place called Vogue Café, the theme here is unadulterated fashion and, in a city where Fashion TV rules supreme, things are not being done by halves. Low level, scarlet velvet seating, set off by black lacquered wood and burnished silver columns, is very much in the lie back and chill mode – so much so that the banquettes come with headrests, so you can tilt your head to optimum cocktail sipping angle without tiring out those neck muscles unduly. Giant canvasses offer a witty homage to Botticelli, with Venus, newly born from her scallop shell, clutching an ipod in a classic little red dress, with a smear of lippie in the latest must have scarlet. The crowd is also a chilled 25-35 set, dressed to the nines and sipping their cocktails like there is no tomorrow.

snack...

Baku is mercifully free of the international evil empires of coffee, although this does mean it can be hard to find a decent cup and, with a cappuccino setting you back somewhere in the region of 4-6 AZN, this can be as expensive as it is frustrating. The Baku Roasting Company (BRC) is the only place in the country – and probably in the whole Caucasus – to roast its own beans and serves up an excellent cup of coffee done any which way. Best bets closer to downtown are Ali & Nino, Aroma, both Azzas, Café City, all of the Chocolates, Dondurma, Hazz and La Vita, while The Gourmet Shop at the Hyatt is pretty much the one and only in the Nasimi area.

Tea is, of course, where it's at for Azeris and the ubiquitous 'Çay Evi', or tea house, signs will testify to that. Tea is drunk black, often with lemon and always served with a wide array of sweets – sugar lumps, bonbons, preserved or dried fruits, chocolate, honey, jam – and is usually sweetened by sipping at the unsweetened drink over something sweet held in the mouth, rather than stirring it in as we would in the West. Tea with jam or quince in honey is a great pleasure and well worth departing from western convention to try. The best tea places in town are Kishmish in the Old City, the Hayat Çay Evi up near the Hyatt, as well as the unnamed tea house atop Martyr Hill (see Culture), and Mirvari Café (not to be confused with the Park Inn's Mirvari Bar) on the Boulevard. Also worth a brief mention on the Boulevard is the (unreviewed) Veteran Café near Government House (Dom Soviet), where old men gather daily and play a very photogenic game of backgammon.

The ultimate snack food in this part of the world is, of course, the kebab. *Kebablar* actually cover a wide range of dishes, some of which are more stew than skewer, but if it is spitted meat on the hop that you are after, then you want a *schaorma* and

you could do a whole lot worse than the imaginatively named Schaorma No 1 on Nizami Street, where you should plump for a *lavash*, which refers to the bread wrap – a sort of fluffier, thicker take on pitta bread. *Qutab* (Gutab) are the other great Azeri snack – a folded Mexican-style tortilla, filled with spiced meat or greens – and available everywhere.

If it's international goodies you crave, then check out Pizza Holiday or the US Diner and Tex-Mex joint Sunset Café. There are sadly golden arches in Fountain Square (and Ganjlik district) and frustratingly – as elsewhere in the East – there is perceived to be a certain depressing caché to whiling away an afternoon at Mac-cyD's, in plain sight of the passing crowds. Ice cream lovers will melt for Dondurma and chocaholics will follow suit at any of the Chocolate Cafés, though Aroma's hot chocolate gives them a serious run for their money. The Chocolate Cafés and Aroma are also two of the very best for desserts – a national pastime here – along with Azza, the BRC, Fashion Café and The Gourmet Shop at the Hyatt. Health freaks are generally not so well catered for, although one great exception to that is the Vitamin Bar at the Landmark, whose fresh juice and smoothie menu will leave you champing at the all-organic bit.

On those sweltering summer days, you'll need to catch every breath of breeze you can and your cool spots and hip hangouts for that are on the Dalida terrace above Fountain Square, the Vitamin Café at the Landmark, Mirvari on the Boulevard or up on Martyr Hill.

Wireless internet is almost everywhere, although the signal can be patchy, so be aware you will share your snack-time with facebookers hunched urgently over their laptops – yes, Facebook is in Baku in a big way.

Ali & Nino Café *(top)*
Café – Z. Taghiyev St, 16/18
Book Café – Nizami St, 19
Torgova
Tel: Café - 493 15 30
Book Café – 493 93 68
www.alinino.az
Open: daily, 10am–11pm

Named after the eponymous lovers in Kurban Said's great masterpiece of Azeri literature, written in Germany, The Ali & Nino café and A&N book café are a pair of quiet havens off the bustling crowds of, respectively, Fountain Square and Nizami Street, that serve up excellent coffee and pastries and, in the case of the café especially, a very good light lunch. The café is opposite the adults' and children's bookshops of the same name (and management) while the book café is located in the basement of the other branch of the bookshop itself. The café has been sensitively decorated in an elegant, period style to reflect the novel's setting – the first years of the twentieth century, when Baku was at the height of its first oil boom. Literature geeks may even notice that the broken clock downstairs is set to 5.15, the precise time in the novel at which Ali meets his... well, that'd be telling.

Aroma Café *(left)*
Uzeyir Hajibeyov St, 18
Torgova
Tel: 598 07 70
Open: daily, noon–midnight

The Aroma Café is a light and breezy breath of fresh, coffee-scented air just up the street from the always manically busy Sahil Metro station. Serving Illy Coffee, excellent, thick hot chocolate and delicious pastries to eat here or take away, the Aroma is popular with a wide mix of people. Courting couples head for the tucked away recesses of the first floor room, while more boisterous groups of youngsters follow them upstairs, but tend to stay out in the open on the more visible sofas. Downstairs is more the domain of young families, who congregate on the more accessible tables. They offer a full menu of light lunches, including soups, salads and sandwiches and a tea list of sixteen different varieties. Staff are friendly and the light jazz soundtrack pleasingly relaxing, no wonder then that in its five years of opening, the Aroma has established itself as a café to be seen in.

Azza Café *(right)*
ISR Plaza: Ground Floor,
ISR Plaza
Fountain Square: Islam Safarli St, 1
Torgova
Tel: 498 24 02 (ISR) www.azza.az
Open: daily, 6–10am, noon–11pm

Can the Azza group do no wrong? With a well-established chain of patisseries and the bar and restaurant at the top of ISR Plaza, that service the Radisson Blu Hotel, you'd be a fool to overlook perhaps their greatest works – the Azza Cafés at Fountain Square and at the foot of ISR Plaza itself. Design here is impeccable – Fountain Square, with its gorgeous summer terrace overlooking the Square, is all billowing white canopied ceilings and signature panels of mirrored DPM. Over at ISR Plaza,

snack...

things lean towards a more restrained, classic style, but with a smacking great Azza twist – think black and silver printed fabric lampshades and flock-etched mirrors, accompanying plushly upholstered deep, comfy sofas and chairs. The real stand-outs for all this design success, though, are the desserts. As beautiful to gaze upon as they are delicious to gobble up.

 **Baku** *(left)*
Roasting Company
Alasgar Alakbarov St, 12
Yasamal
Tel: 510 98 76
Open: daily, 9am–9pm

The brainchild of American ELT teachers Dina and Dan, who decided that they needed a second business to sit alongside their English School and lamented the difficulty they had in finding a decent cup of coffee, the Baku Roasting Company is the only place in Baku to roast its own beans. You can buy the beans – and a plethora of other caffeinalia, including affordable French presses/cafetieres – whole or ground, as well as brewed up into whatever takes your fancy, perhaps accompanied by a slice of their awesome pumpkin cheesecake. The lively café functions as much as a community centre for the English language students as coffee shop, and the management also holds regular non-profit making exhibitions of photography, arts, handicrafts and the like. Plans are also afoot to market the beans through other outlets and even supply coffee wholesale – so watch out for the BRC logo.

 Café Balizza *(right)*
Nizami St, 83
Torgova
Tel: 498 88 71
Open: daily, 10am–11.30pm

A handy pit-stop on bustling Nizami Street, The Café Ballizza, with its wall-mounted, 24/7 Fashion TV and blow up posters of models on the stairs, could just as easily be remodelled as a fashion café but, this being Baku, that name had already gone. The upstairs salon is a vision in pearl, gold, brown and taupe, with deep sofas and walls upholstered in a sort of pearlised, snakeskin textured velveteen. Plastic wall lights dripping in cascades of faux-crystal beads complete the look, which somehow works in Baku and what elsewhere might seem a little cruise ship, is remarkably soothing. The menu is better on the salads and sandwiches than the sushi, and the coffee is reasonable. A cut-price business lunch is served, although for the mainly twenty-something clientele, the main draw seems to be endless teas and coffees and the odd beer upstairs.

 Café Caramel *(top)*
A. Ali-Zadeh St, 7
Torgova
Tel: 498 93 53
www.cafecaramel.net
Open: daily, 11am (10am Sat/Sun)–11pm

An always busy new opening in the heart of buzzing downtown, Café Caramel is popular with families and friends taking a mid-afternoon break from shopping at the mid-range stores around Natavan Square, as well as a

later crowd of after-dinner loungers en route between – or even as an alternative to – the many restaurants, pubs and clubs of the area. Downstairs is comfortable and well-designed, but not a patch on the upstairs salon, where great use is made of the vaulted ceiling, with pink-hued lights and waves of frosted glass. The best tables – a couple of intimate comfy chair set-ups – are up here too, accessed across a suspended walkway offering the perfect vantage point for a cup of so-so coffee and an excellent cake or dessert and a few sharp-tongued observations on the passing crowds on Ali-Zadeh Street below.

 Café City *(left)*
Rashid Behbudov St, 8
Torgova
Open: daily, 9am (noon Sun)–midnight 2am Sat/Sun)

Another relative newbie, Café City is large and airy, with hugely high vaulted ceilings, white walls, and walnut wood screens, nicely set off by the odd potted palm. Tables are laid out sparely, with seating on cream banquettes and subtly branded walnut chairs and there is a wonderful feeling of space and room to breathe. The clientele is very mixed, representing all ages and types – some come for a quick coffee, others take advantage of the very good menu of snacks, sandwiches and salads which, unusually for Western café-style establishments in Baku, also includes a good number of national dishes, such as excellent *qutab*. The soundtrack is an excellent chill-out mix, which is also available as a CD for sale over the counter.

 Café Mozart *(bottom)*
Abdulkarim Ali-zadeh St, 2
Tel: 493 19 11
Open: daily, 24 hours

Open since 1992, and thus only months after Azeri independence from the Soviet Union, the iconic Café Mozart is one of the oldest places in town and also pretty much the only one to be open 24 hours. Always busy – ok except perhaps at about 5am on a Tuesday – the Mozart is popular with about as mixed a crowd of mainly locals as you could expect. The pall of cigarette smoke indoors is swiftly blown away by the breeze out on the balmy terrace, where the buzz of phone conversations conveys the probably correct impression that a lot of serious business is done here, as well as, of course, the serious business of resting one's bones from the power-shopping to be found around Natavan Square. The business lunch buffet is especially popular, but the whole menu is good and reasonably priced and somehow feels much more authentic than many of the trendier, newer establishments that surround it.

 Chocolate Café *(right)*
Mammadaliyev, 4, Torgova
Tel: 418 11 27
Landau St, 535, Husein Javid Ave
Tel: 510 69 87
Boyuk Gala St, 21, Old City
Tel: 492 35 26
Kichik Gala St, 124, Old City
Tel: 437 32 21
Open: daily, noon–midnight

The Chocolate Café chain, now numbering four establishments across the

city and with Cio Cio San (see Eat) making up five, is a wonderful little empire, richly deserving of its success. Each café has its own signature decorative style, but generally is along the lines of a chic, classic, 'Parisian-café-with-Eastern-twist' feel. The exception to this is downstairs at the Husein Javid Ave branch (actually on the south side of the square), which is much more electro-disco, reflecting its popularity with the bright young things of the nearby university, but don't worry the ground floor here is just as refined and elegant as the others. Husein Javid and the newer Old City location at Kichik Gala also have a more extensive, restaurant-style menu, but all serve up the most wonderful hot chocolate concoction of the melted choc of your choice whisked into hot cream. Chocaholic heaven.

Dalida Café   (bottom)
3rd Floor, Nargiz Mall,
Fountains Sq, Torgova
Tel: 496 88 04
www.dalida.az
Open: daily, 10am–3am

True, the Dalida Café does not necessarily look much more than a fairly generic shopping centre café, but step out on to the terrace and it is immediately apparent why it has made the Hg2 grade. When the stifling heat of summer lies stagnating in Fountain Square below, you'll catch every available breath of air up here, all the while enjoying an excellent cup of coffee and a range of the usual snacks, salads, sandwiches and sweets, or a more substantial option from the next door restaurant, which shares the same outdoor space. A great place to escape the shopping crowds below and enjoy one of the city's best views. But you don't have to take our word for it, just look around you – this many shoppers, students and groups of families and friends can't be wrong.

Dondurma   (top)
Filarmonia Park, near Old City
Metro, Old City
Open: 11am–midnight

Entering the Dondurma Café it is a good idea to keep your eyes up. The white, wrought iron furniture and columns, the plate glass windows giving on to the wonderfully geometric shapes of the cypresses and clipped box bushes of Filarmonia Park beyond have all the charm of a peaceful Italian piazza, to say nothing of the grand backdrop of the Old City and the Louvre-like glass pyramid of the new Old City Metro. Why then, one wonders, did they feel the need for such garish leopard-spotted tiles? Dondurma, meaning simply 'ice cream' in Azeri, source their rich and creamy wares from Italy and the ice cream, served on and in the usual range of waffle cones and tubs and so on, is superb. Add to that excellent crêpes and other desserts and wonderful coffee, made from a carefully crafted house blend, and one can easily forgive the odd strangely orange feline spot or two.

snack...

Duplex Café *(left)*
Mirza Ibrahimov St, 1
Torgova
Tel: 494 99 90
www.duplexcafe.az
Open: daily, 11am–11pm

Just a few paces off the north side of Fountain Square, Duplex is a new opening that reminds you just how great it is to be in a city where coffee chains don't exist. As the name implies, the interior is laid out over two floors, with the upper salon making great use of the low vaulted ceilings as an architectural feature. Lighting is pleasantly low, décor restrained and the space is great. Popular with students and a generally younger crowd poring over their textbooks, discussing reading lists and, er, updating their Facebook pages. In summer, there are plans for an outdoor terrace, stretching out across the sunny street and looking down over Fountain Square. With good coffee, a varied and well-priced snack and light lunch menu and this position, it looks like Duplex will make its mark.

Fashion Café *(right)*
Gogol St, 3
Torgova
Tel: 493 03 98
Open: daily, 10am–midnight

Just a couple of steps away from the main mid-range shopping stretch of Nizami Street, with this position it is no wonder that in the 18 months or so that it has been here The Fashion Café has built up such a crowd of regular customers – for the most part weary shoppers resting their aching pins without having to flex their credit cards. Red velvet banquettes and a lot of mirrors predominate in what is perhaps more Heat magazine High Street style than Vogue magazine Milan couture, but the effect works notwithstanding. Coffee is fine here, but a better pull is the list of 16 teas and, even more so, the excellent range of tarts, pastries and other desserts, all made on the premises and lip-smackingly good. The management can be a little on the frosty side, but hey, that's fashion sweetie and the waiters will charm.

Gümüs Maska *(bottom)*
Young Spectators' Theatre,
Nizami St, 72, Torgova
Tel: 417 66 68
Open: daily, noon–11pm

Gümüs Maska, or the Silver Mask, is a tricky one to pin down. With an excellent full menu and a decent cocktail list to boot, it was a strong contender for inclusion in the Eat and Drink chapters, but its popularity with a lunchtime crowd and some great salads and sandwiches won through for Snack. Situated on the top floor of the Young Spectators' Theatre, it is a vision of modern architectural design – all steel girders, high-tension wire edged walkways and plate glass – and looks wonderful, shimmering on a bright summer's day. Service is good, if a little formal, and the clientele, not as theatrical as one might expect from its location, is a mixed bag of folk from ladies lunching in between shops to the odd couple on a snatched lunchtime assignation via a smattering of besuited gents from nearby offices. Something for everyone then.

snack…

Hazz Café *(bottom)*
Landmark Rotunda Square,
Nizami St, 90, Torgova
Tel: 598 29 78
Open: daily, 7am–midnight

Tucked into the ground floor of the Landmark Building – the same building as some of Baku's premium office space and the British Embassy – and accessible from within the Rotunda Square as well as the street on the other side of the building, it is no surprise to find that the Hazz Café is bustlingly busy on a daily basis from dawn to dusk, with its mainly suited clientele. Service can be a little slow on occasion, but the coffee is excellent, the breakfast buffet varied, the business lunch very popular – although quality can be variable – and the lunchtime harpist an unusual draw. The walls feature some interesting modern art canvasses and choice pieces of wonderful traditional textiles and clothing, conjuring up a relaxed but sophisticated vibe.

Hayat Çay Evi *(right)*
Bakikhanov St 17
Nasimi
Open: daily, 11am–3am

Just along the block from the Russian Embassy and on the corner of Bakikhanov and Gardashlar, the long-established Hayat *Çay Evi* (or Hayat Tea House) is one of the relatively few remaining open-air terraces in town. A great place to sit in the sunshine and enjoy a cuppa (*chai*), with all attendant sweets, or a pint (*piva*) or three in a heavily Azeri-accented atmosphere. There is a good menu of home-made

Azeri snacks and light bites on offer, though be prepared and come armed with a phrase book, as very little Russian and almost no English is spoken here. The friendly staff will flash their gold teeth at you in a willing smile, however, and respond well to pointing, grinning and, especially, taking their photo, and it does make a very refreshing change from all the usual ex-pat haunts.

La Vita *(left)*
Istiglaliyyat, 31
Old City
Tel: 497 52 20
Open: daily, 9am–1am

La Vita enjoys one of the better positions in this part of town and a wonderful view out over the glitteringly controversial Louvre-esque glass pyramid of the new Old City Metro. The ground floor is popular with the odd suited meeting and plenty of young mothers and their buggy-bound progeny, while in the comfortable environs of the upstairs salon, clad in golden flock wallpaper with sumptuously decadent red satin banquettes, younger groups jockey for the best seats by the windows, which overlook the Metro square, and are the perfect spot to spy on the comings and goings of that cute guy/girl from their economics lecture. The menu is good, if leaning a little towards the more substantial than the surroundings perhaps call for, so despite palatable pizza and pasta, one can't help but wish for a scrumptious salad or sandwich.

Marco Polo   *(left)*
Khagani St, 17
Torgova
Tel: 493 31 32
Open: daily, 9am–midnight

When Café Vanilla closed its doors, many regulars went into mourning, but when Marco Polo threw open its doors on the same spot a few months later, most of them were more than happy to transfer their allegiance to this comfortable and welcoming alternative. A convenient location a block from busy Bul-Bul to the east and Nizami to the north, Marco Polo is set back from the street under a portico, with a great south-facing terrace for the regular clientele of families, couples and businessmen to take their al fresco coffees or partake in an excellent light bite of lunch. The elegant interior is hung with reproductions of engravings from Marco Polo's voyages, which led him through Baku some 800 years ago. Ask nicely and the friendly waiters will even show you a copy of his illustrated travels, complete with a short chapter on Baku back then.

Mirvari Café   *(bottom)*
Boulevard, near
Museum Centre, Torgova
Open: daily, 6am–2am

Far and away the best of the Boulevard cafés, the Mirvari Café (not to be confused with the Mirvari Bar in Drink) is instantly recognisable by its undulating wave of a concrete roof, lending it – though only from certain angles – an almost Sydney Opera House-like silhouette, albeit in a smaller and more concretey way. Ok, it's really not much like the SOH, but it is undeniably distinctive. The raised floor catches every breath of breeze on those stultifyingly hot days, while the signature roof provides a very welcome shade. If the wind gets up, however, then you can always retreat to the lower level, where you stand a decent chance of some shelter, as you sup a beer or partake in something from their decent, if not outstanding, menu. Open late in summer months, it is also a popular post-prandial spot for a digestif.

Papillon   *(right)*
Gogol St, 8 (Molokan Gardens)
Torgova
Tel: 498 98 22 www.papillon.az
Open: daily, 11am–midnight

Entirely unrelated to daring escapes from Devil's Island or to French lepidoptera, Papillon is a very pleasant café/restaurant/bar situated in the Molokan Gardens on the former site of the Shakespeare Pub (now round a couple of corners on Ali-Zadeh Street). The salon is a long room in a comforting shade of pinkish red, dominated by a Deco-style wave of pink recessed lighting, which does lend a certain fine, Frenchy feel, that is no doubt in part behind the concept and name. Small framed prints of street scenes and still lifes compound the effect and a relaxingly laid-back lounge soundtrack makes for a comforting and somehow discreet atmosphere. The seating is, in the main, in booths, the perfect place to share one of their killer desserts and gaze longingly into one another's eyes, as many of the youngish crowd seem

more than happy to do.

Pizza Holiday *(left)*
Lermontov St, 119, Old City
Tel: 497 37 72
Open: 10am–10pm. Closed Mondays.

When Montana native Anson and his Russian wife Tanya moved to Baku over 10 years ago, there really wasn't much in the way of decent pizza. Tanya was looking for something to keep herself occupied, so they started experimenting with different dough proving techniques and trying out the results on their friends. The friends loved it and the rest, as they say, is history. Four years on and the Pizza Holiday family are doing a roaring trade, very much deserving of their well-earned rest on Monday's day off. The pizza, as NY-style dictates, is wide, thin-crust, foldable and melt in the mouth tasty. The trick, says Tanya, is fresh, well-rested dough and their special sauce – a secret recipe, natch. With takeaway delivered in special thermo-bags sourced directly from NYC, it is easy to see why this is Baku's preferred pizza.

Schaorma No. 1 *(right)*
Corner of Nizami St
& Gogol St, Torgova
Open: daily, 10am–midnight

Few of the many open air terrace bars, cafés and restaurants in the centre of town survived the great – and arguably misguided – city-wide clean up of the early 2000s. One welcome exception is Schaorma No 1, which to the uninitiated might look like just another local version of a dodgy, international fast food joint. The reality is that, for all of about one single, solitary, lonely even, Manat, you can get a superior kebab, or *schaorma*, wrapped in delicious fresh *lavash* bread with all attendant toppings and, in a town where top tucker usually costs top dollar, this is not something to be sniffed at. Authenticity-seekers can wash this down with an *ayran* – a popular local yoghurt based drink, not unlike salty *lassi* – but the local beer is also good and reasonably priced here, if you're not feeling quite so adventurous.

Sunset Café *(bottom)*
M. Rasul-Zadeh St (in the Cinema building facing onto the Square), Torgova
Tel: 492 22 92
Open: daily, noon–11pm

From the same management as the excellent Scalini (see Eat) and The Lounge (see Drink), The Sunset Café is a Baku institution. Located in a hard to miss spot on the side of the – sadly, now all Russian or Azeri language – cinema. The ever-busy Sunset Café is also one of the most popular meeting places in town with groups of young-uns, families and ex-pats, in fact a crowd that pretty much represents every social group in town. With a spot-on diner and Tex-Mex menu; Hollywood mug-shots and movie posters plastered all over the bare brick walls and the odd screaming neon sign, it looks the part as much as it tastes it. Wednesday night is Tex-Mex extravaganza, though the bowls of steaming hot, spicy chilli; burgers and all day breakfasts hit the spot on any day of the week.

The Gourmet Shop *(top)*
Hyatt Regency, Bakikhanov St,
1, Nasimi
Tel: 496 12 34
www.baku.regency.hyatt.com
Open: daily, 11am–7pm

Recently re-opened after the 2009
renovation of the whole Regency
property, The Gourmet Shop has
proved itself a huge hit with ex-pats
and guests alike. With a menu of
mainly soups, salads and a build your
own sandwich concept (for a fairly
hefty 10AZN, though they are admittedly very good), it is always busy with
a mainly foreign crowd. Coffee is by
Illy and brewed to perfection, especially good when chased with a couple of the very fine home-made truf-
fles. The Gourmet Shop also serves
as an excellent deli, with a small but
excellent, seasonal selection of oils,
wines, cakes and luxury items in tins
and jars from around the world and at
a premium. For the budget-conscious
luncher, by the way, a good tip is to
take a brace of the very tasty side-sal-
ads, which will fill you up for a fraction
of the cost.

....

Vitamin Bar *(bottom)*
The Landmark Hotel, Nizami
St, 90, Torgova
Tel: 465 20 00
www.landmarkhotel.az
Open: daily, 10am–midnight

Attached to the Landmark Hotel's
excellent Health Club up on the 9th
floor, the Vitamin Bar – and especially
its sun terrace – is one of the best
pulls in town, enjoying spectacular
views across the city, above the hustle
and bustle of street level. The mooted
external staircase, linking indoor pool
with sun loungers and due to open in
2010, will only enhance its already stel-
lar reputation. Open to guests, health
club members and, crucially, also walk-
by customers, the sun trap terrace
and impressive range of freshly made
juices and smoothies and carefully-
designed menu of energy-giving, im-
mune-boosting salads and sandwiches
lend a welcome healthy edge to your
lunch, but they are so tasty you don't
feel like your skimping on the pursuit
of pleasure we hedonists live by. If
you've never tried it, the khurma juice
(persimmon or sharon fruit) is a delicious, oozingly honeyed must!

Face Club

party...

The news in late 2009 that a certain well-known travel publisher had publicly declared Baku the world's 8th best party town was greeted by Bakuvians with a derisive snort. The truth is that, while certainly a very relaxed and tolerant one, Azerbaijan is a Muslim country and high-octane partying and Islam do not sit well together. Having said that, get under the skin of any city and you will find there is fun to be had and Baku is certainly no exception. The best resource on what's hot in town is online listings site www.citylife.az. Here you'll find out about any one-off parties held by private promoters as well as what's on at the established places. Many of these one offs take place in private hire venues like Abu Arena – a fair distance from the city centre – or Buta Palace, which is even further afield, outside Baku itself and off the airport road.

Back in town, all talk at the moment is of the imminent arrival of the World Fashion Lounge on the site of much-missed dual concept Asian restaurant Taboo/Yin-Yang, opposite Government House. Launched in official partnership with that great Bakuvian obsession, Fashion TV, WFL looks set to take on current hipsters' favourite Face Club for the coveted crown of Queen of the Bakuvian night. Another hip pretender to that throne is the recently re-opened (and in a new location) Metkarting – a more egalitarian place, where cover charges are generally lower and the crowd a little less exclusive. Multi-functional Chinar Lounge is also set to become a fave nocturnal haunt, though perhaps more for the lounge-lizard than the party animal. Time will tell.

Along with Fashion TV, karaoke is the other great Bakuvian party-going obsession, as it is pretty much everywhere on the globe stretching from here to the East. Karaoke is offered by many bars, some restaurants and even in the flashier suites

Metkarting

of some hotels, but the best places in town for atmosphere and for the staggeringly large choice of songs are indisputably Pride and the Studio 2.

When Le Mirage closed its doors in 2009 Baku lost its first, last and indeed only ever gay bar. Homosexuality was decriminalised in Azerbaijan in 2000, although openness and widespread tolerance are still a fair way off. Generally, there is no gay scene, per se, and things tend to operate very much on the down-low. Some venues in the downtown area, such as the Living Rooms 1 (see Drink) and 2 (see Party) are gay-friendly, but any public display of affection would be frowned upon, to put it mildly.

The downtown area is dotted with clubs accessed down dark and often dingy-looking steps and we have descended them all, so you don't have to. Many of these look, and in fact are, rather insalubrious and operate as little more than knocking shops. Although rarely, if ever, dangerous – Baku is a very safe city – there are countless stories of bad situations developing should you choose to book a hotel with one of the lovelies found therein. A word on prostitution: As one might expect in a Muslim country, prostitution is absolutely illegal. That being said, many (though emphatically not all) of the ladies who frequent the bars and clubs of the downtown area may be of somewhat easy virtue and, if paying for it is your thing, you very likely won't be disappointed. Just exercise caution.

Drugs are similarly illegal and very unlikely to be encountered either. Likewise gambling, despite the architectural tradition of such iconic buildings as the Filarmonia, is illegal and there are no casinos in Azerbaijan.

Black Jack *(bottom)*
Bul-bul Pros, 16
Torgova
Tel: 055 757 99 56
Open: daily, 9pm–5am

As the management put it: 'It's the same old Black Jack, just a new place'. Black Jack has been plying its punters with booze for 13 years now, making it one of Baku's oldest nightspots, although it has been at its current location for only the last couple. At first glance it's just another underground dive – laser light shows; variable music policy; sometimes quiet, sometimes rammed; pool table out back. Look a little closer though and you will find very friendly management and a more convivial atmosphere than much of the competition. Even the extremely friendly good time gals perched at the bar will try and hit on you with a knowing, wry grin. Generally busy at weekends, if you feel like slumming it some, then Black Jack is one of your best options in the downtown area.

Chevalier *(left)*
Grand Hotel Europe, Tbilisi Pr, 20,
Nasimi
Tel: 490 70 90
Open: 10pm–4am (6am Fri/Sat)
Tues–Sat

A rather large club with a kitschy medieval knights in armour theme and a logo that reminds of a certain boy wizard's book and movie franchise, Le Chevalier is tucked underneath the Grand Hotel Europe, run by the hotel's management and accessed by steps down the side of the hotel's main reception. It has been a mainstay of the Baku scene for some years now, despite in recent years being extremely and increasingly variable on every level. Music policy varies wildly from night to night – as does the make up and size of the crowd, often according to which large groups are staying in the Europe or, to a lesser extent, the Hyatts down the hill. Like the Europe above, there is something a little past its best about Le Chevalier, but having said that, when the planets – and other variables – are aligned it's one of the most fun nights out in town.

Chinar *(right)*
Shovket Alakbarova St, 1
Sabayil
Tel: 492 08 88
www.chinar-dining.com
Open: daily, noon–12.30am (1.30am Fri/Sat)

Baku's newest and most opulent restaurant and nightclub, Chinar, is situated on the site of an old tea house under a cluster of plane trees, although there's little evidence of its antiquity now under the expanse of glass that boxes in this contemporary monument to the country's booming oil trade. Chinar is not the place to go for underground grooves, but if you want to watch wealthy Azeris at play, then there is no finer theatre in the whole country. Located near to a statue of the mythical Azeri hero, Bahram Gur, Azerbaijan's answer to Saint George, who was sculpted slaying a dragon, he provides the aesthetic inspiration for much of the 1,500 square metre interior of the club, which has a deeply oriental flavour. The club has all the accessories of opulence –

party...

sushi bars, champagne bars, wide screen TVs showing digital art, private dining rooms and superb food from a team imported from Hakkasan in London, as well as the obligatory late night sounds – but it's also open during the day for Baku's answer to tea and cakes for the ladies who lunch, walking their Louboutins and international hairdos. This is the place where glamour and glasnost collide, and the result must be seen to be believed.

Crossroads (right)
Razul Rza, 30, Torgova
Tel: n/a
Open: daily, 11pm–3am (8am Fri/Sat)

What do you do when you come stumbling drunkenly out of the Corner Bar (see Drink) at closing time on a Friday and are in the mood for some ear-drum perforatingly loud rock and, perhaps, hanging with some crazy, mildly aggressive dancers from, say, Sweden or the Czech Republic? Why, pop across the road to Crossroads, of course. Open until very late, serving up beer at pub prices and with a pool table downstairs, Crossroads is extremely popular with a generally younger Azeri and international crowd of students and some of the less aged oil and hotel industry workers. Music is actually pretty variable and some dance or hip-hop may well squeeze its way in between the rock. All in all, it is, weirdly, surprisingly good fun. Door staff are not the friendliest, however, and not averse to upping the arbitrary cover charge if you appear drunk or credulous.

Face Club (left)
Nizami St, 10,
Torgova
Tel: 497 44 71 www.face.az
Open: 11pm–3am (5am Fri/Sat).
Closed Mondays.

Celebrating its first birthday in March 2010, Baku's premier nightclub, Face, has added a splash of Muscovite glamour to Bakuvian nights out. With an excellent, if expensive, nouvelle cuisine menu in the upstairs restaurant; glam interior and lighting design; boomingly clear sound and a suitably snooty door policy, it really is like Moscow at its nouveau heights. They even stop the music and play Eye of the Tiger when someone splashes out 1,100AZN for a bottle of Cristal. Cover charges are complex and, for a foreigner, can range from nothing to 60AZN but are usually around the 20-30AZN mark. We would advise calling ahead, fixing a price and getting your name on the door. If sitting, there is a minimum spend per table of 100AZN and 10AZN per person service, which equates roughly to a bottle of imported spirits, mixers and perhaps a shot or 3 on the side. Again, tables are best reserved ahead, while bar-space is free. Face also plays host to some of the coolest acts in town, recent live shows have included Moscow's premier hip-hop act Basta and a range of jazz-fusion and electronica artists, mainly from former Eastern bloc countries.

Indigo (bottom)
Tarlan Aliyarbeyov St, 6
Torgova
Tel: 493 70 93
Open: daily, 11pm–2am
('til late Fri/Sat)

party...

127

Another relative newcomer to the downtown scene, Indigo will celebrate its first birthday pretty much as we hit the shelves in May 2010. Downstairs is a large, dramatically lit hall, dominated by a pair of huge chandeliers and a massive indigo clock. Up on the mezzanine, things are more cosy and a youngish crowd of students and their friends browse Facebook on laptops and gossip, sorry, 'make observations'. During the week the focus is on a dining crowd here to enjoy their very reasonable, if not exactly stand-out, mid-range menu, but it's at the weekend when Indigo comes alive when the tables are pushed back to make a dancefloor and the resident DJ spins a mix of 80s and electronica, with the inevitable Bakuvian red herring thrown in for good measure. Theme nights, occasional live music and a regular masked Mafia Game (see Play) also take place. Find them on Facebook for more details.

 Infiniti *(bottom)*
Vidadi St, 148,
Torgova
Tel: 596 32 29
Open: daily, 10pm–6am

If you have ever wondered how that baby deer feels as the pack of hungry wolves circles it, drawing inexorably closer and closer, then you'll have some empathy for the foreign male in Infiniti, beset by a bevy of Bakuvian beauties, available for a price. Men stand fixedly, like rabbits in headlights, while the women prowl – usually in pairs – before moving in for the kill. They strike Playboy poses in your sight-line, tossing tousled manes of hair, seductively licking a finger or trailing it in their cleavage, or they do walk-bys, making curious, low, guttural moans or even, in some extreme cases, lean heavily against you at the bar. Anything, in fact, short of actually striking up a conversation. Annoyingly, for some at least, Infiniti consistently plays some of the best dance music in Baku and is arguably the best place to come and get down, if, that is, you can handle the predatory ladies of the night(club), which to be fair are actually the main draw for some of the crowd.

 Jazz Centre *(top)*
Rashid Behbudov St, 19
Torgova
Tel: 493 99 41 www.jazz.az
Open: daily, 6pm–1am
(music from 9pm)

Baku has a long history with jazz and the Jazz Centre is one of the city's most happening weekend party places as well as being a cultural highlight on the music scene in general. There is a nightly live music programme from 9pm until close, but it's at the weekends where things really come to life, with an innovative programme that may include live bands riffing with scratch DJs, swapping singers and generally having all the infectious fun that a good jazz night should include. DJs between acts keep the atmosphere alive with an eclectic mix of jazz, funk and groove classics. Jazz legends such as Herbie Hancock, Al Jarreau have performed here and even George Benson showed his face when he was headlining at the higher profile Heydar Aliyev Palace (see Culture). Food is so-so, so eat first, as it's the music you're here for. Look

party...

out also on their website for forthcoming festivals and events.

Khalifa *(right)*
Rashid Behbudov St, 17,
Torgova
Tel: 498 92 96
Open: daily, 5pm–2/3am ·

Stepping down from the street into Khalifa transports you into the world of the 1001 Arabian Nights. You half expect to encounter Ali Baba peeking out of an oil jar, or Aladdin rubbing his magic lamp. Sadly, these images are just fantasy but if you're after Arabian dancing you're in the right place. Slip off your shoes and sink into a low, luxuriantly upholstered banquette, sip on a cocktail or an expertly served glass of tea, poured from an elaborate metal pot, warmed over candles. Tea comes with preserved quince and baby '*iablochki*' apples, perhaps, or the choicest dates and figs. Marvel at the exquisite frescoed scenes of Arabia, draped in chiffons of every hue under the sun. Then, your senses wrapped in goosedown comfort, the nightly belly-dancing performance starts. Private dances – and note, they are just dances – for one or more can be booked in the separate VIP room.

Living Room 2 *(bottom)*
Nizami St, 34
Torgova
Tel: 495 43 62
Open: daily, 3pm–6am

On the site of the former Le Mirage – Baku's one and only self-proclaimed gay club, that was shut down in 2009

due, oddly, to the apparently unseemly behaviour of the women who frequented it, rather than anything lewd the boys may have got up to, Living Room 2 is the rather unimaginatively named second outfit from the guys at Living Room 1 (see Drink). Again, the interior design concept is over the top Bakuvian boudoir, with leopard print and gold set against scarlet and smoked mirrors. Like its sister bar, it's super-friendly and, again, like its sister bar, also gay-friendly. Living Room's cocktails may be a little rough around the edges, but the atmosphere is top-notch. There is a regular Mafia game (see Play), live music on Saturdays and a DJ the rest of the weekend, playing upbeat tunes. Look out for notices outside and posters around town about forthcoming events and specials.

Metkarting *(left)*
Aliyar Aliyev St, 1993
Narimanov
Tel: 564 33 32
Open: daily, 11am–7am
(club from 7pm)

When the old Metkarting closed its doors back in 2005, a generation of Bakuvians shed a collective tear. Towards the end of 2009, however, the all new, improved Metkarting mark two was unveiled at a brand spanking new location and featuring a shiny, all new go-kart track, with shiny, all new (and disturbingly speedy) go-karts, an outdoor area, with sun loungers, plunge pool and a beer terrace and, crucially, Baku's biggest centrally located nightclub. The club is a glorious temple to all things kitsch, with a chessboard floor, mirror balls – and mirror walls

party...

– white leatherette banquette seating, neon signs, pop-arty canvasses and staff in gold and silver lamé shirts. The sushi is good, the music is straightforward, accessible poppy dance and MTV classics, special themed nights are on the up and the drinks are at an ok price – so far, so potentially very good indeed. What remains to be seen though, is if they can pull in enough of a crowd to fill this huge venue come summer-time. We seriously hope so.

Opera Lounge *(bottom)*
Izmir St, 9, Nasimi
Tel: 418 06 60
www.operalounge.az
Open: daily, midnight–2/3am

A year old now, the Opera Lounge has effortlessly established itself as one of Baku's hippest venues since it opened back in May 2009. More lounge bar than its clubbier competitor Face, Opera is all about louche comfort – deep sofas in warm, comforting coffee and cream, set off by mood lighting and mauve highlighted pillars. Fashion TV plays on plasma screens throughout, fortunately with volume down so you can appreciate the musical offerings, which include a nightly live jazz set from their excellent house band, as well as live acts and guest DJs from all over Europe, playing a wide range of styles. There is also a proper fine dining setup, serving excellent – if pricy – food from European and Japanese menus and a small but serviceable dance floor. The management also runs one off events, such as karaoke with live band accompaniment, both here and at other larger venues in and around town, which they promote heavily with posters and flyers around town and on citylife.az and their own website.

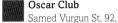

Oscar Club *(top)*
Samed Vurgun St, 92, Nasimi
Tel: 597 04 05
Open: daily, 7pm–2am

Managing to combine Hollywood gangster chic with a 1940s sultriness, the Oscar Club lounge bar and restaurant oozes pure, but relaxed, glamour. A palette of cream and brown is lent a note of colour by table top red carnations. walls are adorned with framed black and whites of Oscar winners and UV-lit fish tanks and yet still manages somehow to look understated. The party vibe is chilled here, though when there isn't live jazz going on, music courtesy of MTV Dance keeps the atmosphere upbeat. The private room is an homage to Pacino's gangster flicks and, appropriately enough, their weekly Mafia game (see Play) is among the most popular in town. It's like a generous measure of LA Confidential and The Godfather with a sprinkling of Fabulous Baker Boys and, while Michelle Pfeiffer may not be draped seductively across this white baby grand piano, it's likely you may find her framed somewhere on the wall.

party...

 Pride Lounge *(left)*
Tarlan Aliyarbeyov St, 9
Torgova
Tel: 493 53 08
www.pride.az
Open: daily, 7pm–5am

Karaoke is big business in Baku and nowhere do they take it more seriously than at the Pride Lounge. Newly refurbished to celebrate its recent first anniversary, Pride is split across two floors. The ground floor is all sparkly midnight blues, deep purples and gunmetal greys, that twinkle under the lasers like a big old disco lounge. There's even a stage with a spot rig controlled by the DJ, so you can take your X Factor fantasy one step further and belt out a blinder with an audience. Downstairs is filled with outsized, stripy three piece suites and an alarming riot of red, orange and yellow floral print wallpaper. Pride promotes itself big, with special nights, such as the recent fashion and beach parties, weekly special cocktails,

look out for fabulous watermelon or mandarin mojitos and singing contests to win membership, which equates to discounted drinks and other perks, like priority in the queue to perform.

....

 Studio 2 *(middle)*
Uzeyir Hajibeyov St, 4
Torgova
Tel: 598 42 41
Open: daily, 7pm–5am

Beneath a Japanese restaurant on the South side of Molokan Gardens, Studio 2 is a popular basement karaoke bar and chill out club, deservingly well known for its opulent shows, which have included belly dancing, fire breathing and snake dancing, one can only hope and assume not at the same time. The large main saloon features splendid fish tanks as table bases and a rouched, canopied ceiling, while gold, silver and bronze VIP rooms are available for private hire. Different parts of

the bar are separated by heavy, sound-proofing curtains, so fear not, your cat-erwauling won't throw the singing sen-sations in the next room off their beat. A good, solid and reasonably priced menu of sushi and light bites is on of-fer and with over 20,000 songs in more than ten different languages on the list and a further 15,000 on the computer, you can be pretty assured of finding a tune to wow the crowds, whatever your musical taste.

Twins Lounge *(right)*
Khagani St, 41,
Torgova
Tel: 055 677 44 88
Open: daily, 2pm–6am

Swishing your way up the impressively sweeping Deco steps to the front door, it is easy to imagine you have 'arrived', as you gracefully enter the Twins Lounge. A glance around the seduc-tively mood-lit room at the well-heeled,

dressed up, late night crowd, lounging in velvet bucket seats and swirling ma-tured cognacs around their expensive crystal balloons will likely confirm that, while you may not have done, they certainly have. As the night progresses, the heavy blinds on the plate glass windows at the front lower, until you will feel for all the world like you are at a speak-easy during prohibition. The mood here is very much dictated by the crowd, and if you happen to be in when chemistry dictates a party, this is the swingingest joint in town. At other times, the low-level, laid-back chill-out sounds provide the perfect backing to a gentler affair.

culture...

Baku is a city whose culture is best imbibed wandering through its streets, and nowhere in modern Baku is this truer than wandering around the streets of the Old City and the faded grandeur of the nineteenth and early twentieth century boom-town that lies around it. In terms of cultural highlights, hidden within the Old City are gems like the unique Shirvanshah Palace, the iconic Maiden Tower and the impressive walled defences of the city. The other outdoor cultural highlight is the affecting cemetery and monument up on Martyr Hill, formerly known as Kirov Park. With its stunning panorama across the whole city, this is a must by day or night.

Around the Old City, lies the heart of the nineteenth and early twentieth century oil boom-town, with some stunning examples of gloriously over the top oil baron palaces, notably the Wedding Palace and the Hajinsky Mansion. Some, like the Taghiyev Mansion, now house museums. Around these, and especially to the immediate west of the Old City, lie some less grand examples of the period, which have a distinctly European feel to them, like a dilapidated grand old district of one of Europe's grand old cities, such as Paris or Budapest. Among these also are the ultimate in crumbling glory – Fantasia Baths.

Baku's museums are housed in some impressive buildings, but their contents can be somewhat disappointing, when placed next to the tons of gold leaf, vast marble fireplaces and astonishing chandeliers of the palaces themselves. Notable exceptions to this rule are the State Carpet Museum and the Azer-Ilme Carpet Factory, both of which are very much worth a visit. Also impressive is the small portion of Shahid Habibullayev's private collection of Azeri metalwork currently on display within the Shirvanshah Palace until it finds its new home in a private dedicated museum. This is rumoured to be on the site of the current Carpet Museum, which is due to move to grander new premises at some point in the next couple of years. Most museums have a two-tiered pricing scheme, with locals getting in for less than a third of foreigners.

Big news on the art scene is the planned new Museum of Modern Art, which has such big names attached as Pritzer Prize-winning architect Jean Nouvel (of Barcelona's mini-gherkin, the Torre Agbar fame) and former Guggenheim director Thomas Krens. Nothing is confirmed yet, but comparisons to Bilbao's world-famous Guggenheim Museum have already been made in the press. For now though, a thought-provoking collection of 800 pieces by Azeri artists has been brought together at last year's new opening, the Museum of Modern Art. On a smaller scale, the privately run, non-commercial Kichik QalArt (Kichik GalArt) and the privately run commercial gallery, Gyz Galasy hold some interesting exhibitions in the Old City of promising, up-and-coming and more established artists.

On the music front, big names who pass through Baku tend to play either the Heydar Aliyev Palace or, in summer, the Open-Air Concert, or Green Theatre. The Face Club (see Party) also plays host to some hip names and famous faces, mainly, though not exclusively, from the Moscow scene. Jazz is massive and the jewel in the crown is definitely the Jazz Centre (see Party), though other venues have good house jazz bands, such as Opera Lounge (see Party) and Azza Bar (see Drink). Rockers should head to the ex-pat pubs, notably the Corner Bar (see Drink), while folksters should swing by Finnegans on a Wednesday or Saturday (see Drink). Classical music is extremely well represented, largely organised by and at the Filarmonia, with large-scale orchestral and operatic festivals running throughout the year. Traditional music is Mugham, primarily at the all new International Mugham Centre, which organises an annual Mugham Festival, details of which are on the Centre's website, and the Mugham Club, where you can partake in a fine dinner too.

There is currently no English-language cinema in Baku.

Tickets for all major events are available from the venues themselves, as well as from ticketing kiosks at Rasul-Zadeh St, 3 (outside Café Mozart) and Bulbul Ave, 19 (near the Stock Exchange and Mango flagship store).

Sightseeing

 Bibi Heybat Mosque *(left)*
on Bayil road,
south east of city
Open: 24 hours daily

The Bibi Heybat mosque was a casualty of the Soviet's destructive regime and has now been entirely rebuilt. A stunning and absolutely huge mosque, it is worth a visit and best viewed when lit up by night, perhaps after a visit to the excellent nearby Khazar fish restaurant (see Eat) or at dawn, en route to the mud volcanoes and stone carvings of Gobustan (Beyond Baku, see Play).

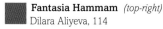 **Fantasia Hammam** *(top-right)*
Dilara Aliyeva, 114
Torgova
Open: daily, 7am–10.30pm

Probably the best example of faded Victorian era glamour in Baku, the ornately tiled and mirrored Fantasia is a must to stop by for a cup of tea and, if you are feeling brave, have a vigorous steam and massage in one of the 23 tiled and rather shabby private rooms. The private rooms are here as this was, back in 1880, the first western-style hammam in Baku, allowing men and women to come and bathe at the same time. Look out for the

ornate tiles in the main communal tea room, which depict hunting scenes and are dated 1896 as well as the group of regulars who will be more than happy to pose for a photo. Outside, the crumbling grandeur continues, with several of the stone lions on the corners of the building rather symbolically missing some of their teeth.

sky Mansion is also one of the few to have been sensitively restored to all of its original glory. This is also famously where de Gaulle stayed in 1944 on his circuitous route to Moscow for his summit with Stalin while still leader of the French Resistance, a fact commemorated by a bas relief on the wall of what now houses the Tom 'Gucci' Ford flagship store.

....

(bottom-right)

**Hajinski
Mansion**
Neftchilar Pr, 103, Torgova

One of the richest of the turn-of-the last-century oil mansions, the Hajin-

Maiden Tower *(top)*
Neftchilar Pr
Tel: 492 83 04
Open: 10am–6pm. Closed Sundays.

Little is definitively known about Baku's most famous landmark, the eight storey high Maiden Tower, with walls five metres thick, which is clearly a fortress, but whose precise purpose, history and the reasons for its name and shape are shrouded in mystery. There is a list of far-fetched stories surrounding its construction, which was certainly no later than the 12th century, but believed by many to go back to the 7th or 8th. The most popular, but by no means most likely, of which concerns an unfortunate maiden, imprisoned by a despotic king – in some accounts her incestuous father – hell-bent on marrying her. Agreeing to marry the despot/father upon completion of a tower in her honour, she inspected the finished work, climbed to the top and hurled herself to her death in the waters of the Caspian, which at that period came right up to the base of the tower, thus preserving her maidenhood and giving the tower its name. A more likely history of the name is that maidenhood symbolises the impregnability of this impressive fortress, which accounts also for the several other Maiden Towers across the region, notably in Istanbul. The building's curious cross-section – like a teardrop, or the stylised flame motif found in a good deal of traditonal Azeri textile-work - resembles a Zoroastrian fire symbol that is tied in to their fire worship, but does this make the tower a definitively Zoroastrian construction? Noone is entirely sure.

Martyr Hill *(bottom)*
Top of Funicular Railway

At the top of the old Soviet curiosity, the Funicular Railway, is the former Kirov Park, now designated Martyr's Alley, Martyr's Lane or Martyr Hill. Here is the immensely moving, understated row of some 130 marble slabs each inscribed with the name, dates and an etched likeness of one of the 130 or so Baku citizens who lost their lives in the massacre by the Red Army on January 20th 1990. At the end of the alley is an impressive tower that houses an eternal flame, burning in their honour. It is an astonishingly powerful memorial and a must-see in Baku. On the slope below the alley, lie further graves of heroes who perished in their thousands in the Nagorno Karabakh conflict. There are splendid views across the city from atop this hill both in sunny weather and at night, and a tea shop that serves tea, with an array of sweets, but pretty much nothing else.

Palace of Happiness
Corner of Murtuza Mukhtarov St & Ahmad Javad St
Old City
Open: 10am–5pm. Closed Mondays and Thursdays.

The most popular of the Baku 'Wedding Palaces' – literally popular mansion venues that can be hired for weddings – the vast Palace of Happiness, with its ornate pseudo gothic spires, scrolls, twirls and flourishes, to say nothing of its rooftop statuary, is something of an architectural wedding cake in its own right. Built by oil baron Mukhtarov as a love gift for his

second wife, whose courtship has become synonymous with romanticism in Baku. Mukhtarov was low-born, exceptionally wealthy and infatuated by the high-born daughter of a prominent aristocrat. When his petitions were resolutely refused, he embarked on a long and careful campaign involving building mosques in her hometown to demonstrate his piety and dependability. The aristo finally relented and, once married, the ever-romantic Muhktarov continued to shower his wife with touching gifts and tokens culminating in this enormous mansion, until his tragic death at his own hands after failing to defend his wife's home against the Communist invaders.

Museums & Galleries

 Carpet Museum
Museum Centre, Neftchilar Pr, 123, Torgova
Tel: 493 66 85, 493 05 01

Open: 10am-6pm. Closed Mondays.

Situated in the huge building of the Museum Centre, the Carpet Museum holds over 6,000 carpets, around 20% of which are on display at any given time. Carpets are organised by weaving style and geographical provenance and cover all of the 144 different types as catalogued by the great Azeri carpet scholar Latif Kerimov, after whom the museum is named.

 Museum of Literature *(above)*
Istiglaliyat St, 53, Torgova
Tel: 492 74 03
Open: 11am–5pm. Closed Sundays.

The Museum of Literature is housed in the former Metropol Hotel, which was the Grand Hotel of Baku until it was closed down by the Soviets back in 1940, and is not to be confused with the new Metropol Hotel (see Sleep). Probably the most photographed building in Baku after the Maiden Tower, its facade, especially when lit up by night, with its alcoved statues of the greats of Azeri literature is unmistakable and frankly stunning. The museum is dedicated to the great luminaries of what is a highly literary society and features room upon room of statues, portraits, manuscripts and artefacts relating to the literary greats of Azerbaijan, although many of the names will be unfamiliar to foreign visitors.

Museum of Miniature Books
Gala (Qala) Lane, 1, Old City
Tel: 492 94 64
Open: 11am–5pm. Closed Mondays and Thursdays.

A wonderful Bakuvian quirk, The Museum of Miniature Books does exactly what it says on the can and features the private collection of bibliophile Zarifa Salakhova's 6,000 odd miniature books, published in over 60 countries and collected over more than two decades. In addition to the best-known names of Azeri literature – Nizami, Nasimi, Khagani et al – the collection also features works by great international writers, such as Shakespeare, Pushkin and Byron, as well as perhaps the world's least convenient reference section of not exactly user-friendly dictionaries and the like.

Museum of Modern Art
Yusif Safarov St, 5, Khatai
Tel: 490 84 02/04 www.mim.az
Open: 11am–9pm. Closed Mondays.

Making a huge impact on Baku's art scene is the brand new, Jean Nou-

vel designed, Museum of Modern Art. Based on the success of the Guggenheim in Bilbao and capitalising on the city's status as the Islamic Culture Capital in 2009, the museum is designed to showcase work of contemporary Azeri artists. The collection houses over 800 works, ranging from sculpture and installations to painting and photography taken from the 1940s onwards. Azerbaijan is now establishing itself on the international arts scene producing spectacular pavillions at the Venice Biennale. The building itself is well wortha visit on its own.

Mustafayev Art Museum
Niyazi St, 9
Old City
Tel: 492 57 89
Open: 10am–6pm. Closed Mondays.

Housed in two buildings just down the hill from the Presidential Office – photography of which is strictly forbidden – and opposite the Filarmonia, the Mustafayev Museum houses a mixed bag of Arts fom across Europe. The lower of the two buildings is a nineteenth century Dutch oil mansion and is home to a not exactly awe-inspiring collection of minor works by some big name artists and is interesting more for the building's interior, than any significant artistic treasures. The upper building – a former school – contains a more interesting collection of Azeri work and is home also to the odd travelling exhibition, such as a fascinating recent show of Oriental textiles in association with the Victoria & Albert Museum in London. In the courtyard behind are some bullet-ridden busts, rescued by chance from a Tbilisi scrap-

culture ...

yard where they ended up after being shot up and looted by Armenian invaders in their original home of Shusha, the main town of the Armenian-occupied province of Nagorno Karabakh.

 Gyz Galasy Gallery
Gulla St, 6, Old City
Tel: 492 74 81
www.qgallery.net

A small commercial gallery in the Old City, which specialises for the most part in twentieth century painting and sculpture – and some photography – by some of Azerbaijan's most famous and most promising up-and-coming artists. The Gyz Galasy, which is the Azeri name for the Maiden Tower, has also teamed up with artists of other nationalities, such as German, to put on exhibitions of dual relavance to the two countries in question. An interesting place and well worth a brief stop on a tour of the Old City.

 Shirvanshah's Palace *(top)*
Boyuk Gala St, 46
Old City
Tel: 492 10 73
Open: daily, 10am–7pm

The stunning complex of the Shirvanshah's Palace is the greatest cultural draw of the Old City and dates in the main from the 14th and 15th centuries. Incorporating the Shah's palace, mausoleum, personal mosque and hammam, it is a stunning example of medieval Islamic architecture and home to some quite simply breathtakingly ornate Islamic carved stonework and tranquil courtyards. The central,

vaulted hall is currently home also to a small portion of the impressive private collection of eccentric philanthropist Shahid Habibullayev's amazing array of rescued and Azeri metalwork and other artefacts, all personally restored by Shahid himself. Among the collection is the personal phaeton of the Nobel family, rescued as an anonymous rusting hulk from a rubbish tip in Sheki. There are hopes that the collection of some 3,000 pieces will soon find its own home in a private museum.

Performance

 Opera *(bottom)*
& Ballet Theatre
Nizami St, 95, Torgova
Tel: 493 16 51

Although currently closed for renovation, the Opera and Ballet Theatre – named after the great Azeri playwright Akhundov, known as the Moliere of the Caucasus – is still worth a mention as one of the most curiously beautiful buildings in Baku. Surprisingly, it has retained its charm even post-renovation, after it was gutted by fire back in the 1960s, and also has a wonderful story attached to its construction. Snubbed by Baku's greatest opera singer of the time (1910) the fabulously wealthy Mailov Brothers resolved to build something even more stupendous than the brand new mansion the singer had been showing off. When a visiting Russian soprano, Nezhdanova, said she would not return to a city whose wealthy populace were not philanthropic enough to build a splendid opera theatre, the Mailovs had their goal set and resolved publicly to build an opera theatre worthy of Nezhdanova's charm and talent within a year. Fellow oil baron Taghiyev doubted the feasibility of such a build and accepted a wager to pick up the tab, should the works over-run. 10 months of triple shifts later, the opera theatre was built and Taghiyev out of pocket to the tune of 250,000 roubles, a stupendous sum for the time. When Nezhdanova played to a full-house at the opening gala, notable among the few non-invitees among Baku's high society was the opera singer who had previously snubbed the brothers.

Baku State Circus
Samad Vurgun St, 68, Nasimi
Tel: 494 90 23

As elsewhere in the former Soviet Union, the circus tradition is a strong one in Azerbaijan. This is the official home of the Baku State Circus and also plays host to other touring companies, such as the Moscow State.

Filarmonia   (top)
Istiglaliyyat St, 2, Old City
Tel: 497 29 01
www.filarmoniya.az

A stunning vision in a Floridian combination of pastel yellow and white, the Filarmonia building looks like a giant, edible fondant fancy. The Filarmonia was originally built back in 1910 as a casino and modelled on the great gambling houses of Monte Carlo. The story goes that it was modelled after a design, sketched with a cigar stub in a moment of inspired genius by the suitably hedo-

nistic-sounding architect. Impressively renovated back in 2004, The Filarmonia Society puts on an impressive array of classical concerts in the indoor main hall, the smaller rotunda in the park and on the impressive outdoor stage (which rumour has it was built facing the mansion that now houses the Mustafayev Museum after a hefty bribe from that building's then owner).

Heydar Aliyev Palace (middle)
Bulbul Pr, 35, Torgova
Tel: 498 81 84
www.ha-saray.az

Baku's premiere music venue, formerly known as the Lenin Palace, Baku Palace and Republic Palace, the Heydar Aliyev Palace was renamed after the late former president on his death, by his successor and son, current president Ilham Aliyev. It seats around 2,000 and, after recent renovation, in some comfort too. It is the place to see the biggest names visiting town which in 2009 included jazz-soul legend George Benson and Kelly Rowland, formerly of Destiny's Child. Situated on the square facing the National, or Milli Bank, which sports a wonderful polished marble floor – great fun for pensioners in icy weather – and an iconic statue of Heydar Aliyev himself.

International   (bottom)
Mugham Centre
Boulevard Park, opp Funicular, Old City
Tel: 437 00 30 www.mugam.az

Azeri Mugham – a traditional style of narrative folk music – was recognised

HEYDƏR ƏLİYEV SARAYI

culture...

by UNESCO in 2003 as being one of the 'Masterpiece of Oral and Intangible Cultural Heritage of Humanity' and in 2008, the International Mugham Centre opened to celebrate *mugham* and all its variants, which are found across the Middle East. The undisputed jewel in the crown of recent architectural arrivals on the Baku skyline, the unmistakable organic lines and upright pillars of the Mugham Centre are best appreciated when lit up by night for one of the impressive concerts. The foyer contains busts of some of the great *mugham* artists of now and yesteryear, but it's the unique sound and moving rhythms that will stay with you after as you appreciate what is a uniquely Caucasian and especially Azeri tradition and sound.

....

Mugham Club   *(left)*
Hagigat Rzayeva St, 9
Torgova
Tel: 492 40 85
Open: daily, 5pm–midnight

As listed also in Eat, The Mugham Club is in an unusual two storey caravansera – most in this part of the world are strictly one storey affairs – which dates, in part at least, from as far back as the 6th century and is thought to be where Marco Polo stayed when he visited Baku en route to China in the late 1200s. The friendly stall-holders upstairs are your best bet for a quick guided tour (and don't feel obliged to buy either). At one point this caravansera was linked by tunnels to the small one being excavated up the street and the well-known Caravansera restaurant (see Eat) on the other side of Maiden Tower. This linkage provided much-needed escape routes in times of siege. Look out for the larger corner suites of rooms, which were reserved for dignitaries including, most likely, Marco Polo, and the steps up to the upper storey, which have been re-cut to be half their original height. Unconquerably high steps being another weapon of defense in the besieged forces' arsenal. As well as the cultural heritage of

the building, the *mugham* concerts and dance displays that take place nightly during dinner are an excellent way to pop your *mugham* cherry.

 National Academic Theatre
Fizuli Square, 1
Torgova
Tel: 494 48 40
www.azdrama.az

The impressive colonnaded façade of the Milli Theatre, or National Academic Theatre, is the ancestral home of Azeri thespdom, an artistic discipline with a wealth of history and tradition behind it. Here you will find lengthy classics played out in Azeri or, occasionally, Turkish language but, in truth, little to interest all but the most ardent foreign theatre-goer. The National Theatre Museum, situated in the same building as the Carpet Museum (see page 142) is similarly for die-hard aficionados only, as much due to lack of familiarity with any of the major players in Azeri

theatrical history as anything else.

 Open Air *(right)*
Concert Theatre
(Green Theatre), Istiglaliyyat St, Sabayil
Tel: 492 49 82
Open: summer months

Reopened following renovation in 2007 after more than a decade of disuse had seen it fall from 1960s iconic venue into an a parlous ruined state, The Green Theatre – or Open-Air Theatre – as it is more familiarly known, plays host in the summer months to some of the bigger name visitors to Baku's stages, in recent years including such leading lights of the Turkish music scene as multi-platinum selling artist Tarkan and Eurovision contender Hadise Acikgoz. Among Westerners who have graced the stage here in the last few years are, er, the cast of ABBA the musical.

culture...

Puppet Theatre
Neftchilar Pr, 36
Old City
Tel: 492 64 25
www.kuklateatri.com

In its prominent position a short hop down from Maiden Tower, right on the Boulevard, made more so by impressive night-time flood-lighting, the Puppet Theatre is one of Baku's most visible theatrical establishments. Although aimed primarily at children, the shows are charming and extremely well-performed by stunningly able puppeteers. Unfortunately for most foreigners, most shows are performed in Azeri and the few foreign language ones tend to be from around the region – in Russian, Farsi or Turkish – but with some shows very familiar, such as Aladdin and various works by Hans Christian Andersen, the language difficulty is often surmountable. If you are lucky and hang around after the show, you may also be allowed a fascinating glimpse at the intricate workings back-stage too.

Russian Drama Theatre
Khagani St, 7
Torgova
Tel: 493 40 48
www.rusdrama-az.com

In its unmistakable scalloped white glory, the Russian Drama Theatre is another very recognisable Baku landmark. Its current guise is its third, it was originally a stunning piece of mock-chinoiserie called the Mikado Theatre around the turn of the last century and then an uninspiring dark behemoth until its current reconstruction in the 1950s. While the National Theatre concentrates on works in Azeri, the Russian Drama Theatre focuses more on international greats by such leading names as Chekhov, Tennessee Williams, Arthur Miller, Lope de Vega, Somerset Maugham and, of course, Shakespeare. Works are all performed in Russian but the spectacle – and talent – is undeniable even to foreign ears. A children's programme also runs here, with shows like The Nutcracker laid on for a packed family crowd that often fills Khagani Street outside at the interval.

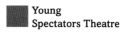

Young Spectators Theatre *(right)*
Nizami St, 72
Torgova
Tel: 493 88 52

In a modern building of steel and reflective glass that divides opinion among architectural critics, but is undeniably successful with its interior (see photo of the stunning in-house bar-café-restaurant The Gümüs Maska, in Snack), the Young Spectator's Theatre runs a programme of events aimed at pre-teens and teens. Notable more for its controversial architecture, made more so by its position opposite the old-school charms of the Opera-Ballet, than anything of great interest to the adult spectator.

culture...

shop...

Walking along Neftchilar (Neftchilar) Prospekt, admiring flagship after flagship of some of the world's most famous – and most expensive – fashion brands, you could easily be forgiven for thinking you were in Milan, or one of the other acknowledged world fashion capitals. A closer inspection, however, will reveal that pretty much every one of these stores is pretty much empty of customers pretty much all of the time. The simple fact is that most of these boutiques are kept alive by a single customer (presumably not the same one) coming in once a month or so and blowing around $50,000 in one splurge. Yes, the choice is there, but prices do not compare favourably to Europe and, unless money really is no object, you may prefer to wait until you get home before picking up that Little Black Dress. That being said, last season's items can often be picked up at around 50% discount, and it is practically altruistic to give all those bored-looking, glamorous shop assistants something to do trying things on. On the mid-range budget, fashion is very much centred around Aziz Aliyev and Razulzade Streets, while the main drag of Nasimi is mainly filled with rather unexciting Turkish and Azeri brands which are cheaper, yes, but do have a tendency to look it.

The Azeri carpet and woven textile industry is one of the country's most important ones and it continues to develop and strengthen. A visit behind the scenes at the Azer-Ilme carpet showroom and factory (see Culture) will give you a good idea of just why the price tag on many of these carpets is so astronomical – this is seriously labour-intensive work. Most carpet shops will also sell a variety of other antiquities and traditional handicrafts. Traditional hats make a great gift, although be aware that a shaggy shepherd's hat costs around a third what it does in Baku (c. 50AZN) if bought where they are made – up around the Sheki area in Northern Azerbaijan. Copper work is another traditional handicraft and a trip to the pretty mountain village of Lahij, the village where the bulk of it is made in traditional workshops, is one of Baku's most popular day trips (Beyond Baku, see Play), but don't expect a much better price at source.

There is a cluster of carpet and antiquities shops around the Maiden Tower and others scattered around the Old City, but if you want to buy, or even just browse carpet styles and other antiques over a pot of tea, there are two places we would recommend above the rest for their friendly and non-pushy owners – Brothers Carpets in the Old City and Sheyk Safi in the downtown area.

The shops around Fountain Square are, as we go to press, a rather unexciting bunch of rather drab fashion boutiques and ubiquitous mobile phone outlets. As Fountain Square is due to reopen following extensive renovation in May 2010, there is talk of raising the shopping profile around here too, so watch this space. To the Eastern end of Fountain Square are the well-known book and art alleys, which

Deutsch Apotheke

shop …

are worth a browse and certainly photogenic. Stalls selling all manner of tourist chooch, antiquities and Soviet memorabilia abound, but haggle hard, as opening prices are often laughably high.

Most of Baku's bazaars are eminently practical affairs, selling foodstuffs and household items in the main. Far and away the most atmospheric – and photogenic – is the Taza Bazaar on Samed Vurgun Street, at the junction with Asgarova Street. Do be aware of unscrupulous dodgy caviar salesmen though. A word on the (other) black stuff, it can be hard to source good quality caviar that will turn out actually to be, er, good quality caviar. If you do want to take some home, be aware there is an export limit of 125 grams per person and it must be factory packed. Caviar costs around 20-30% what it might cost in the West, but you will still pay around 100AZN for 125g. Excellent quality caviar from a trusted source can be arranged by the management of Paul's restaurant (see Eat).

Far and away the best selection of English books is available from the Ali & Nino bookstore on Nizami, and their other branch on Taghiyev Street in the downtown area. Valonia, also on Taghiyev, and Patchi on Nizami Street are two outlets for very high end chocolates. The Gourmet Shop at the Hyatt Regency (see Snack) is also worth a mention for their chocs and stocks a small but good range of other luxury foodstuffs too, albeit at a premium. The Azeri wine industry is coming up and now producing some fine dry reds. Ismailli Wines and the Ibrus Wine Club, both in the Old City, will sell you a bottle, or case, of surprisingly good stuff, while the nearby Wine City will give you a taster of what import taxes mean it costs a local to put European wines on the table.

Supermarkets are variable in Baku, with the various branches of Continental particularly iniquitous on pricing – up to 15AZN for a packet of everyday coffee, for example. The MUM store is an unremarkable old Soviet era behemoth on the North side of Fountain Square, opposite the Ministry for Internal Affairs. There are five Baku branches of the popular Ramstore in town, two of which crop up regularly in directions – one is near Husein Javid Square and the Baku Roasting Company (see Snack) is located directly behind it. The BRC, incidentally, is the only place in Baku to buy a cafetière, or French Press, at a reasonable price. A second, larger Ramstore, is on the airport road at Khatai Avenue, near the Excelsior Hotel (see Sleep) and Shilla Korean restaurant (see Eat). Citimart on Samed Vurgun is also generally thought to be one of the better bets, along with the New World supermarket a block down Izmir Street from the Hyatt.

A last word. Pharmacies are everywhere in the city, identifiable by a neon green cross. English is widely spoken and most medicines are freely available, for a price. One pharmacy, however, deserves special mention for its astonishing interior design concept, featuring huge, whirring, under-floor cogs and a robot pharmacist. The Deutsche Apotheke on Aziz Aliyev Street is pure Alice in Wonderland and will have you reach for your camera quicker than you can say White Rabbit.

shop …

Brothers Carpets

Along Boulevard

Neftchilar Prospekt
From the East, starting near the junction with Niyazi Street

81 – Paul & Shark preppy casual wear for men and women with a nautical theme from Italian mid-range label

83 – Pal Zileri Italian designer suits and boots

85 – Marina Rinaldi womens wear from the Italian Max Mara group, aimed at the more curvaceous figure

87 – Gant large flagship of the Scandinavian American preppy favourite for men, women and kids

89 – Albatros mid-high range suits and accessories for men, with branches located all around the city

89 – Corneliani middle of the road Italian suits and semi-formal wear for men

89 – Moreschi dress shoes and formal accessories from the mid-range Italian label

89 – Ermengildo Zegna flagship of the super-stylish Italian suit-maker

91 – Armani Junior outfitter of choice for every self-respecting oligarch's child

91 – VIP ART mens' shoes and accessories boutique, with products from a wide range of well-known designers, including John Richmond

91 – Karloff high end jewelry boutique

103 – Tom Ford one of the best locations in town – ground floor of the Hajinski Mansion – for designer turned some time film-maker Tom 'Gucci' Ford

103 – Gianfranco Ferré formal wear with a pared down sophistication from the one time Creative Director at Dior

105 – Celine French fashion house of classic women's wear

105 – Dior the last word in classic French style

117 – Dolce & Gabbana the flagship store of the Italian luxury super-brand and Azeri favourite. As we go to press, a second store is due to open imminently, around the corner on Aziz Aliyev Street.

117 – Gucci enormous flagship for the world's biggest selling Italian fashion label

119 & 121 – Salvatore Ferragamo three branches of Florence's finest shoes, bags, accessories and extravagant ladieswear

125 – Burberry English classic tailoring from the revamped Grand-daddy of Classic Brit style

131 – Versace Versace's first Baku flagship was still behind hoardings as we went to press. Expect something huge and eminently over-stated

131 – Karen Millen small but perfectly formed outlet for the British design outfit, now owned by an Icelandic conglomerate and gone truly global

131 – Alma Store the first and only official Apple stockist and repair centre in Azerbaijan

131 – Frette upscale bedlinen – high thread count, natch – and sleepwear

131 – Azza the flagship branch of the Azza group's small chain of patisseries, selling irresistible cakes and patisserie to go

131 – Santorini upmarket men's formal shoes and leather accessories

131 – Avenue rather flashy womenswear designer emporium with a wide range of designers represented – second branch also on Rasul Rza St.

Zarifa Aliyeva St
around the junction with Samed Vurgun Street

21 – Escada accessible high end womenswear and sportswear form the German-based international luxury brand

15 – Etro colourful and wearable Milanese mens and womens fashions with a special emphasis on patterns, such as paisley, and luxury fabrics

10 – Kid's Couture high end designer fashion for the heir to the oligarchy

10 – Liberi yet more unfeasibly expensive kids fashions

Old City

Brothers Carpets
13/6 North Side
Kichik Gala St

Our favourite of the many Old City purveyors of carpets, handiscrafts and antiquities, they also offer a washing, restoration and repair service.

Ismailli Wines
24, Vali Mammadov St

New wine-tasting and selling outfit show-casing the fine wines of the Ismailli region, whose dry reds are very palatable indeed.

Ibrus Wine Club
73, Mirza Mansur St

See also Eat, another new Old City wine specialist, seeking to raise the profile of domestic wine.

Around Old City

Azerbaijan Avenue
(North of Old City)

17 – Apriori very wearable German womens smart-casual fashions

17 – Betty Barclay another German label, offering womens casual wear with a hipper edge

20 – Daniel Hechter Parisian menswear, womenswear and accessories

shop…

West of Old City

Wine City
76, Lermontov Street

Where the self-respecting oligarch comes to pay through the nose for a bottle of average imported wine.

....

Downtown Area

Aziz Aliyev Street
from Southern end

1 – Bulgari ultra-high end jewelry brand which does a fine line in overstated bling for the oil WAGs

1 – Tiffany what is this, oil baron bling corner? Baku branch of the classic New York jeweler to the uber-rich and famous.

2 – Koton preppy, smart-casual fashion for men and women

3 – Trussardi Jeans very contemporary, cool designs from the forward-thinking Italian design house

3 – Caractère middle of the road fashion from Italian label with a large presence in the former Soviet world

4 – Allure mid-range handbags and other comen's leather accessories

4 – Miss Sixty Baku branch of the Anglo-American pop and street-style brand

4 – Guess brand new flagship for the popular US High Street street-wear label

5 – Deutsche Apoteke perhaps the only pharmacy in the world that will have you reaching for your camera, with a glass floor displaying whirring, outsized cogs and the only robot prescription dispenser we have ever seen

5 – Dolce & Gabbana due to open in March 2010, this will be the second Baku branch for what is one of the most popular labels in town

6 – Yeni Gallery small, independent commercial art gallery with some surprisingly interesting art

6 – Max & Co Max Mara's affordable range of casual womenswear

7 – MG Music Store (instruments) the sine qua non for musos, which sells pretty much every imaginable musical instrument known to mankind

9 – MG V Store (equipment) the AV branch of MV, selling all maner of Hi-Fi and hardware

11 – Amazon lingerie boutique selling a wide range of well-known designer lingerie labels, including La Perla, Nina Ricci, D&G and Giorgio Armani

11 – Tommy Hilfiger the flagship branch of US modern legend Hilfiger's affordable casual and smart casual wear

11 – Sabina flagship of the Azeri high end cosmetic and perfume chain, with branches all around the city

13 – Pink cheap and fun bags, belts and other accessories for younger women

15 – University Book Shop huge, sprawling bookshop. Some English language books, though not a patch on the Ali & Nino chain

---

Mammadamin
Rasul-Zadeh St
from southern end

4 – Steilmann good, mid-range mens and womens fashions from the leading German High Street brand

5 – Accessorize one of two Accessorize franchises in Baku, the other being in Fountain Square.

6 – Women's secret mid-range lingerie and women's sleepwear, some of which is hilariously tacky, but some ok

6 – Grand AV Baku's biggets and best music and dvd store

8 – Quiksilver surf and extreme sports casual wear

8 – Mothercare Baku branch of the maternity stalwart, with infant clothing and all manner of baby accessories and paraphernalia

8 – Sisley the preppier, more classic brand in the Benetton empire

14 – Ideal wide range of mid-range cosmetics and perfumes

14 – United Colours of Benetton the brighty coloured, infectiously poppy Italian brand has three branches across the street from one another as well Sisley just along the way

---

Tarlan Aliyarbeyov St

14 – Mexx mens and womens casual, cool fashions from the lading mid-ranger in Germany

---

Zeynalabdin Taghiyev St

10 – Valonia with its name taken from the Wallonia region of Belgium, Valonia is an upmarket chocolaterie, making the finest chocs to Belgian recipes. Also a wedding organiser.

19 – Ali & Nino Bookstore this small Baku chain (the other branch is on Nizami Street) has the best selection of English language books and takes its name from Kurban Said's cponymous classic of Azeri literature

---

Yusif Mammadaliyev St

5 – Sheyk Safi Carpets among the finest carpet and antiquities boutiques outside the Old City

Rasul Rza St
from Southern end

1 – Emporio Armani glitzy flagship store of Giorgio's secondary brand

5 – Cesare Paciotti Italian handmade designer shoes, boots and leather

shop…

accessories for men and women

5 – Prémaman upscale French kids designer clothes brand

6 – Avenue 2nd, smaller branch of the flashy womenswear designer emporium – the flagship is on Neftchilar Prospekt – with a good slection of well-known, high end labels

6 – Aisel womenswear designer emporium with a wide range of high end labels

6 – Brioni Baku branch of the Italian label, once synonymous with Riviera Chic

6 – Miss Blumarine the kids version of Italian label Blumarine

7 – Lacoste French stalwart and proponent of primary coloured polo shirts

7 – Pinco Pallino more very high end kids designer wear

7 – Pret a Porter another womenswear designer emporium with a wide range of high end labels

8 – Canali Italian men's formal and semi-formal wear

8 – Stefano Ricci another upmarket Italian suits and boots outfit

8 – Hugo Boss large flagship store for the German turned international design icon

9 – Bottega Veneta luxury leather goods from a once family-run business, now part of the Gucci empire

9 – Yves Saint Laurent classic Parisian style and a premium

23 – Mango very popular, always busy second branch of the Spanish High Street fashion brand, the flagship store is on Bulbul Prospekt, near the junction with Nizami

Fountain Square

Puma
Nargiz mall (behind McDonalds)

Puma's main presence in Baku is tucked away in the largely unremarkable Nargiz mall. They are also at 8 Behbudov Street, a few blocks West of the Hyatt

L'Occitane de Provence
Nargiz mall
The French purveyor of wondrous potions, creams and other assorted smelly stuff is also at Tolstoy Street

Ecco
Nargiz mall
men's, women's and kids' shoes from the Danish shoe manufacturer whose mission is to combine comfort and style. Also on Hajibeyov St

Accessorize
6 Fountain Square
one of two franchises of the cheap n cheerful accessories shop, the other is around the corner in Rasulzade St

Nizami Street (Torgova)

56 – Ivanovka Market a strange anachronism if ever there was one, the largely unmarked outlet shop for the only still working Soviet collective farm in the world in the village of Ivanovka (see Beyond Baku, Play) sells astonishingly good produce in an atmosphere that is pure, unreconstructed Soviet Union, except that here the shelves aren't bare.

70 – Patchi chocolates super high-end Lebanese chocolates-as-gift store, selling very expensive chocs packed into even more expensive silver and glass objects. Patchi famously teamed up with Harrods a few years back to make the costliest box of chocolates ever.

91 – Ali & Nino Bookstore the second branch of the small Baku book chain has the best selection of English language books in Baku, as well as a free book-swap shelf in the downstairs café

91 – Bata large store of the originally Czech shoe giant with a huge presence across Eastern Europe and on into Central Asia

Around junction of Nizami St & Bulbul Prospekt

18 Bulbul – Adidas reasonable, if not overly impressive flagship for the international sports brand

16 Bulbul – United Sport wide range of international sports brands, separated into sporting disciplines and the only place in Baku to pick up a yoga mat.

19 Bulbul – Mango giant flagship of the Spanish High Street affordable fashion chain which is perennially busy, although not as busy as its other branch on Rasul Rza St

191 Tolstoy – L'Occitane de Provence
second outlet for the high end products and all things perfumed people, whose other store is in the Nargiz Mall on Fountain Square

Nike
corner of Bulbul & Khagani
A large Nike franchise, rather than an actual flagship, this is a so-so outing and real sports fans will be better of at United Sport around the corner on Bulbul

Azza Patisserie
corner of Khagani & Samed Vurgun another branch of the Azza group's irresistible cakes and patisserie to go outfit

Western Downtown

28th May Street
from East at junction with Bulbul Prospekt

2 – Royal Collection a wide range of upmarket jewellery from various European designers

2 – Cartier surprisingly discreet location for the French uber brand of super expensive bling, that needs no introduction

2 – Okaïdi stylish and affordable kids clothing from France

2 – Etam mid-range French lingerie and saucy sleepwear

3 – Ambiance flamboyant crystal and chinaware gifts

5 – Casadei mid-range women's shoes, handbags and accessories

5 – Sergio Rossi more Italian made leather goods for women boots, bags and other bits

6 – Bang & Olufsen state of the art hi-fi equipment and other toys for boys

7 – J-Lo the incomparable Ms Lopez has franchised her brand of street fashion out via Moscow-based Crocus Group, resulting in an impressive Baku flagship

7 – Chopard small but perfectly formed outlet for the very old French form of rarifed, classic fine jewellery

8 – Villeroy & Bosch the last word in luxury tableware from one of the oldest names in the business

8 – Longines very fine Swiss watches with over one hundred and fifty years of experience behind them

10 – Sabine another branch of the high end perfume and cosmetics chain

12 – Baku Electronics electrical goods and kitchenware

Olimpik Star Bowling

Aura Fitness Centre

WALKING LANE

play...

One enormous and pleasant surprise for the luxury leisure-seeker in Baku is the astonishing Sabun Nga Thai Spa, located in a gated compound in an upmarket residential neighbourhood of Northern Baku. From the moment you pass the golden lions flanking the door, you leave all things Caucasian behind and are transported to Chiang Mai, home to the best treatments and massages in Thailand. Chiang Mai is home also for all the smiling staff of the spa, the beautiful decorative touches and artefacts herein and even the very materials that have gone into building this authentic Thai retreat. As you would expect, the international hotels have all the usual sporting and keep-fit disciplines and facilities amply covered, while the ex-pat and Azeri communities also support a range of active and less active sporting and other leisure activity groups.

In a country that is not even two decades independent, it comes as no surprise that there is not the wide range of out-there activities that have been developed over decades in other more established cities around the globe. If you are looking for bungee-jumps and paragliding, then for now at least you are probably looking in the wrong place, but be patient and ask around and you never know. Many sporting activities are organised by ex-pats who have an inevitable tendency to finish their tour and move on to the next posting. The net result of this is that certain sporting clubs and their activities phase in and out of active existence with the passing of time. More and more Azeris are getting involved, however, in more and more of these activities, with the result that the network is becoming more permanent every year. In a scene with such great potential for transience though, the best bet even for a short-term tourist or visitor is to network among the longer stayers. This is easily done through events like the Hash or Ultimate, both listed in the chapter text here. It should be a cinch to find out what is going on this week, or this month, as inevitably activities and events will come and go and establish themselves or drop off, according to demand.

Among the chief attractions for any visitor to Baku is, perversely, leaving Baku. Within easy reach of the city lie a the wealth of fascinating places. Azerbaijan is home to nine of the world's eleven possible climate zones and, from lush subtropical forests in the South, to the icy mountains of the North, via barren, flat salt-marshes and rolling grasslands, there really is a lot of variety to experience. Half of the world's mud volcanoes are in Azerbaijan, a country only around the same size of England, while fire – Azerbaijan means Land of Fire – also plays a large part, with burning mountainsides and even burning springs on the menu out in the provinces. Natural phenomena aside, Azerbaijan's tradition of accepting different ethnicities has led to it being home – now and for centuries – to a wide variety of curious, sometimes ancient communities that the uninitiated would certainly not expect to find in a modern-day Muslim country. A (very) few highlights beyond Baku are listed here, but for anyone with a serious hankering to get to grips with this intriguing country, Mark Elliot's excellent Trailblazer guide to Azerbaijan, with side-trips to Georgia is an absolute must-read.

Far and away the biggest up and coming news on the Baku play platform is the all new ski resort being constructed up North at Shah Dag, near the town of Guba. An estimated two billion US$ is being sunk into the project, construction of which began in 2008 and which will include 21 ski lifts and top-notch facilities for a range of other summer and winter sports. The proposed plan has, inevitably, divided opinion massively, with critics pointing out that with no native culture of skiing and alpinism and, crucially, no mountain rescue service in operation either, the resort is in danger of becoming a massive white elephant. Fans of the proposal, however, point out that more and more Azeris are developing an interest in mountain sports, for which they currently have to travel to Europe. Further, a project of this ilk is exactly what is needed to make use of the country's impressive geography and will give the Azeri tourist industry another much-needed string to its bow that, as yet, is largely based around great untapped potential. We shall watch with interest.

A more modest and, in many people's eyes, more realistic project is well underway 20 kilometres from the ski area, near the town of Gusar. The Hale Kai Mountain Resort is the brainchild of the team behind the Hale Kai Hotel in Baku (see Sleep), who have all skied and skidooed much of their lives as well as trained in avalanche control, mountain rescue and the like. Their planned eco-resort will include cabins and semi-permanent yurt accommodation and activities – in designated, patrolled 'safe' areas – as diverse as cross-country skiing, skidooing, quad-biking, mountain biking, hiking, horse-riding, fishing and wildlife viewing. They are also forging ties with the local communities and will offer cultural tours around nearby villages, which contain over 50 different ethnic groups, speaking 33 distinct languages in this, one of the most culturally diverse regions on the planet. For now, they operate a couple of fairly basic huts, with electricity, heat and running water – no mean feat for the mountains! – and are happy to arrange custom, small group trips for weekends or longer, to include a range of the activities listed above.

Quad biking in the Caucasus

Sabun nga Spa

play...

Beyond Baku

Within a couple of hours of the city centre lies a very different Azerbaijan. Gone is the veil of modernity and European sophistication, to be replaced by a land of primal geography, barren landscapes and simple, village life. English – and indeed Russian – is much more rarely spoken out here, so it is easiest to arrange a driver/translator from one of the travel agencies listed in the info section. So get yourself some wheels and get out and explore.

Absheron Peninsula

If, as it is often described, Azerbaijan is a great eagle, stooping into the Caspian, then the Absheron peninsula forms the giant raptor's beak and Baku's bay the underside of the lower mandible. Around the peninsula are some interesting villages, many with medieval defence towers in varying states of decay, notably old Ramana (not to be confused with the nearby new Ramana). In the unassuming town of Surakhanı lies the hugely significant, if rather underwhelming, Ateshgah Zoroastrian Fire Temple, which dates back to at least the 13th century AD, with some academics claiming this was a holy site for the fire worshippers as long ago as the 6th century. Once upon a time, the holy fire at this temple burned constantly from natural oil reserves, but these reserves ran out in the late 19th century, since when the flame has rather less romantically been supplied by piped gas and these days is largely only ignited for tourists. More impressive, is the burning mountainside at Yanar Dag, which does indeed burn 24/7 from gases produced by the oil-rich soil beneath. Although open all day, it is at night when the sight is most impressive and visitors can take tea and an impressive array of sweets, lit and warmed by the inferno of the flaming hillside.

Beaches

The closest beaches to Baku are at Shikhov (near the Ramada Hotel) on the Salyan Highway to the South West, where you can observe oil rigs on the horizon as you top up your tan, or on the Northern Absheron peninsula at Amburan, Märdäkän and Novkhanı. Better, cleaner beaches, though drab by European standards, are 2-3 hours up the coast North of Baku at the 'glamorous' beach resort of Nabran, where much of Baku repairs when the mid-summer heat gets to be too much, making it a very busy place indeed.

Gobustan

About a 2 hour drive to the South of Baku, past the impressive Bibi Heybat Mosque and on through strangely photogenic and almost beautiful barren oil wastelands lie the prehistoric petroglyphs of Gobustan, inscribed into the World Heritage List of UNESCO in 2007. There is a small park here containing stone carvings that date from the 12th century BC and which are among the earliest and most significant relics of early *homo sapiens* in the world. The park has been recently smartened up somewhat and now boasts a well-signed route, taking in the most significant carvings of men, hunters, animals and pregnant women. A small donation is expected at the gate towards upkeep. Nearby, a Roman soldier, garrisoned here in around 75AD, inscribed a rock

Fire Mountain (Yanar Dag)

Gobustan

Mud Volcano, Gobustan

Kish village

Coppersmith's Workshop, Lahij

Khans' Palace, Sheki

with his name, rank and number which is now protected by a small fence, but open for the world to see. This piece of graffiti is also the Easternmost trace of Roman occupation ever discovered. Azerbaijan is home to half of the world's mud volcanoes – who knew? – and near Gobustan is one of the most impressive crops of them, in a rough ring atop a barren and remote plateau, with views over the Caspian in the distance. The sensation of feeling bubbles of mud rise beneath your feet and erupting in the small caldera is indescribable and, for the record, entirely odourless!

Lahij

The traditional coppersmiths' village of Lahij (or Lahic) is around 2 or 3 hours drive to the North West of Baku and easily doable as a day trip from the city. The village lies at the end of a mountain pass, which can be highly precarious in Winter, when iced or snowed up. En route to the village over a chasm to your right, you will pass a terrifyingly vertiginous rope bridge that even Indiana Jones would think twice about. This is the only access to some very remote settlements, whose inhabitants must carry all supplies from the outside world to their homes across this tiny, swinging walkway. A little way beyond this is a rather broken down looking natural spring right by the roadside, which produces some of the purest water in Azerbaijan – well worth stopping to fill a bottle. Lahij itself is very pretty, with an architectural style entirely of its own and a small and rather pedestrian visitor's centre. Houses here are built in stone, with a horizontal wooden beam every few feet or so within each wall, which acts as a sort of buffer in

earthquakes, giving the building some flexibility and preventing a lot of the damage a rigid structure would incur. Many of the houses here are open workshops, where smiths work copper exactly as they have for generations, producing the pretty copperwork that can often be seen in antique shops in Baku, often with quite a high price tag. It is expected that you will wander in and watch the smiths at work and, should you wish to, purchase anything that takes your fancy straight from the worker himself. If you wish to photograph them at work, it is a good idea to purchase something small from them.

Ivanovka

Near the main road turning to Lahij up on a fertile plain, lies the Russian village of Ivanovka, home to the Molokans, or milk-drinkers The Molokans are a religious sect who believe in worshipping God through tilling the soil and don't worship in churches. They were exiled from Russia centuries ago for daring to protest against their perceived lavishness of the Orthodox Church. When the Soviets invaded it was no great surprise that their style of communal living on a shared farm would appeal and they were designated a collective farm. The surprise came when, after the fall of communism, they elected to keep the Collective Farm, or kholkhoz, and are now the only still working Soviet-style Collective Farm in the world.

Sheki

A six hour or so drive from Baku, the mountain town of Sheki is one of the must-see sights of Azerbaijan. Stay at the eighteenth century caravansera – summertime only, as there is no heating to speak of and winter temperatures plummet! – now a simple but stunningly beautiful hotel, and visit the majestic wooden Khan's Palace, built without a single nail and filled with some of the most impressive stained glass and Islamic miniaturist frescowork in the world today. Nearby is the Albanian church at Kiş (Kish), home to one of the oldest Christian churches in the world, thought by many to be the very first Christian church, as mentioned by St Paul in the New Testament. The Albanians (AlbANNians, no relation to the European country of AlbAYnia) were one of the first Christian civilisations and ruled this part of the Caucasus until around the 5th century AD.

In Baku

Billiards

Although nearly every ex-pat pub in town has a pool table, when they pick up a pole and aim it at some balls, the Azeris are traditionally far more into billiards. The Olimpik Star Entertainment Centre has a large billiards hall with around a dozen tables, as well as bowling lanes, and is open form 10am until midnight daily. It is located at the T-junction at the northern end of Samed Vurgun Street. Tel: 449 40 01

Boat Trips

Boat trips around the bay on reconditioned old hydrofoils leave the Yacht Club pier every hour or so and cost 4 AZN. The round trip takes about 40 minutes and, while there is no commentary and nothing specific to see, it does offer some splendid views of the city and an excellent perspective on the scale of construction city-wide. If possible, sit on the outdoor deck at the rear of the craft for the best photo opportunities.

Bowling

There are two venues for 10 pin bowling in Baku. The Olimpik Star (see Billiards, above) and the Baku Entertainment Centre, a short cab ride to the East of the Government Building, both of which open til late. Lanes usually cost 6 AZN per person, up to a maximum of 12 people on a lane, though this is reportedly negotiable, to some extent. (Baku Entertainment Centre – F. Bayramov Street, 1130/33, tel: 490 22 22)

Cycling

There is an active Baku cycling club which operates a mailing list to put cyclists in contact and publicises large-scale events, including the annual triathlon. Their members also meet for rides within the city, both on the road and at the Velodrome (Velotrek) a mile or so North of the Hotel Europe up on Tbilisi Prospekt. They are also a great resource for finding mountain biking partners for trips around Baku, down to Gobustan up into the Caucasus mountains and operate a mailing list for mountaineers too. See www.bakubicycleclub.com for more details.

Falconry

Falconry – hunting for small game-birds with falcons and other raptors – is arranged in the mountains by the Musado Hunting Club. Unfortunately, they are unable to supply falcons. Most

Bisected Lenin, Yevlakh

play...

of their clients bring their own birds in from the Middle East, where falconry is huge. Email Kenan on musado.hunting@gmail.com for more information.

....

Fishing

The outdoor activities division of the Hale Kai Hotel (see Sleep) is called Hale Kai Mountain Resort and will organise trout fishing in the mountains, as part of an overnight stay at their camp. See "'Mountain Sports' below for more info. The Musado Hunting Club will organise up-country river-based fishing and also out on the Caspian – sadly not for sturgeon, whose fishing is rigorously controlled. See 'Falconry' above for contact information for Musado.

....

Football

Aficionados of the beautiful game can get tickets for games from the main stadium or from the website of the Association of Football Federations of Azerbaijan www.affa.az, which does have a discreet English language button (top right) and gives information about less high profile games and sports grounds around Baku and throughout the country. Mini and 5-a-side football is also played at the newly renovated Bulvar Club, near the Yacht Club Pier and on the Boulevard itself.

....

Golf

Since the closure of the Pink Loch Golf Club, there are now no courses in Azerbaijan, but the annual Azerbaijan Open takes place in Dubai every November. To get on the mailing list, email david@acecaspian.com.

....

Go-Karting

There is a surprisingly impressive Go-Kart track at Met-Karting (see Party), along with a pleasant, if noisy, beer garden and a place to sun yourself by a plunge pool on a hot summer's day. 10 AZN for five laps.

....

Gyms

While there are local gyms at places like the Olimpik Star (see Billiards, above), the best gyms and fitness centres are very much at the better international hotels. Stand-outs among them are the Excelsior's Aura Wellness Centre and The Landmark's Health Centre, both as per listings in Sleep. Also worth a mention is the Hyatt, whose Health Centre is undergoing extensive renovation as we go to press and will no doubt impress.

....

Hammams

(see separate listing for spas)
Most of the traditional hammams are now rather dilapidated and only the brave will be likely to submit to some vigorous scrubbing and rubbing, Azeri-style. Note that English is rarely, if ever, spoken and sexes are forbidden to intermingle, with most hammams being resolutely unisex (usually male) or occasionally open to women, only on certain days. Of those that remain, three of the best are:

The Old City – (Aga Mikhayil) Hammam. Located by the city wall at the Southern end of Kichik Gala St. Men only, except Mondays and Fridays, when it is women only. A bath, scrub and massage will set you back 15 AZN.

A few paces South is another old hammam, which was only rediscovered less than twenty years ago and is now a museum of Herbal Pharmacy with stunning murals.

Fantasia – (D. Aliyeva, 114) built in 1880, was the first bath to be built along Western lines, so entirely composed of private rooms with no communal wash area. For this reason, it is the only hammam that welcomes men and women every day. Now gloriously faded, it is a wonderful place to come and take tea and marvel at the Victorian era grandeur, cracked and stained by years of hard wear. If you are feeling brave enough, a sauna and rub down costs 10 AZN.

Taza Bey – (Sheikh Shamil St, 14) also dates back to the 1880s, but was revamped in the early 2000s and is men only. With décor that has been likened to a theme pub – with deer antlers, Roman Centurions, gilt cherubs and even a rather improbable statue of Charlie Chaplin's Little Tramp – it also costs a rather extravagant 20 AZN for a massage, with entrance and access to the baths and saunas coming in at a far more reasonable 7 AZN.

Hash House Harriers – There are two very active chapters of the Hash House Harriers (aka HHH or H3) – an international collective of unlinked organisations (or perhaps better, disorganisations) who meet and run or walk a marked trail, set by the GMs, or Grand Masters, in a tradition dating back to Malaysia in the 1930s. Originally set up as a means to run off the weekend's excesses, these days the re-

tox social aspect is almost as important a part of the Hash as the detox at the 1,700 or so chapters, or kennels, of HHH worldwide. The very active and sociable Baku Hash is no exception and far and away the best regular event for meeting people and making new friends among the ex-pat and ex-pat friendly local community. Thursdays Hash (Thirstday) is for runners only - email elliott_jc@yahoo.co.uk for more on that – while Sundays meet is for runners and walkers - grandmasterbhhh@gmail.com.

Hiking

Hiking up in the Caucasus Mountains can be arranged by the good folk of the Hale Kai Mountain Resort on hkmr@a-usa.org. There is also a walkers' version of the Sunday chapter of Baku's very active Hash House Harriers (see above), who will be able to put you in touch with fellow hikers, should you wish to arrange a bespoke hike. Be aware that packs of wild dogs are a very real problem in many areas, and groups are often advised to carry stun-guns or cattle prods for personal protection, though a few well-aimed stones should also do the trick. You have been warned. An archived article on the Azerbaijan International Website lists some of the best day trips for hikers around Baku.

Horse-riding

Horse-riding can be arranged at the Hippodrome or by contacting The Gunay Horse Riding Club (Azadlig Avenue, 144A, Tel: 561 91 61/62 www.gunayequestrian.com)

Hunting

The Musado Hunting Club organises groups up into the hills to shoot small game-birds and the Caucasian Tur – a species of large, muscular mountain goat/antelope with an extremely impressive spread of huge horns. You may choose to duck out of the latter trips, as the Tur is now listed as 'near-threatened' and could probably do without tourists taking pot-shots for the sake of a wall-mounted trophy head. See 'Falconry' above for contact information.

Mafia

Sadly an Azeri or Russian language only game, Mafia is something of a Baku obsession and is played in many bars around the city, with each bar usually having a dedicated game night. 12 players sit around a large table and are randomly dealt game cards by the caller, who organises the night. Among the 12 there will be a Mafia Don and his two Mafiosi, a Policeman (Kommisar), a Maniac and 7 clean (or Chisti) people. Players discuss, decide and vote on who they think most likely to be Mafia, which player then attempts to defend themselves. The person with the most votes each round is then bumped off and reveals whether they were Mafia, Chisti or whatever. The Mafiosi try and kill off the Komissar, the Komissar tries to put paid to the Mafiosi, while the Maniac kills with no agenda (and a maniacal cackle, natch). It is all played out to sound effects lifted from the Godfather and, rather surreally, the David Suchet Poirot. A surprisingly large amount of fun, 10 AZN buys you into a game.

Mountain Sports

Mountaineering and mountain biking high up in the Caucasus Mountains can be organised by arrangement with the guys of the Hale Kai Mountain Resort on hkmr@a-usa.org. The actual resort is currently embryonic – just a couple of basic, but well-appointed huts – but is very much a work in progress, with rather grander plans for eco-lodges and cabins afoot. Also worth checking in with the people at The Baku Bicycle Club (see cycling, above) who operate a mailing list of mountaineers and all terrain bikers, allowing you to source, or even form, a mountain-bound group.

Pilates

Currently only offered by the Bulvar Club (see swimming, below) and the Aura Centre at the Excelsior Hotel, as the Hyatt's resident instructor has recently left Baku. It is, however, worth asking at the other Health Clubs – Landmark and Hyatt especially – as they are actively seeking instructors as we go to press.

Pool

Is played at pretty much every ex-pat pub in the downtown area. There are inter-pub leagues too, but casual games – and winner stays on – are the norm on any given night in any given bar.

Quad-biking

The corner-stone on which the Hale Kai Mountain Resort has been built is quad-biking. They currently operate several bikes, with plans also for skidoos to explore the snowy mountains and valleys of Northern Azerbaijan. See 'Mountain Sports' above for more info.

Rugby

There is a surprisingly active rugby scene in Baku under the auspices of the Azerbaijan Rugby Federation. There is also an ex-pat team called The Exiles. For details of the Exiles matches and how to get involved, email John Quinn on john@acecaspian.com or check out the website www.rugby.az

Shooting

See Hunting, above.

Spas

Far and away the best spa experience in Baku and, indeed, arguably also among the best in the world is at the Sabun Nga Spa, recently and deservingly elected to the hallowed ranks of the Leading Hotels of the World's Leading Spas list. Not so much spa as a fully holistic treatment experience, the Sabun Nga will massage your woes away using a variety of traditional Thai techniques in a setting that would not be out of place in one of the many truly world class spa resorts in Thailand. Quite simply stunning Thai design is married with technique that is perfection itself. Your visit is completed by a specially balanced light Thai meal, prepared by their executive chef and served in their private dining suites. (www.sabunngaspa.com). For a satisfying, but more everyday experience, the Aura Wellness Centre at the Excelsior offers a range of treatments, as does the Landmark and Hyatt Health Centres. Both these latter are looking to increase their range of treatments as we go to press, so do contact them directly to find out what is currently on offer.

Squash

The Aura Wellness Centre at the Excelsior and the Hyatt Health Centre both have squash courts available to hire.

Sunning & swimming

Many of the international hotels have swimming pools with sun terraces. Especially popular are the outdoor pools at The Hyatt, Excelsior and Ramada, which has the added attraction of its Caspian beach. The best sun terrace however, despite not having an outdoor pool attached, is the Landmark Health Centre's 9th floor terrace, with truly splendid views across the city.
Outside of international hotel land, the newly renovated Bulvar Klub, near the Yacht Club pier (Tel: 497 04 20) and the Ganjlik Sports & Health Club on Olympia Street (Tel: 465 84 00) are both popular.

Tennis

There are outdoor courts at the Ramada, Excelsior and Hyatt's Health Centres, as well as at the Bulvar Club and Ganjlik Sports & Health Club (see listing for sunning and swimming, above).

Ultimate Frisbee™

Another unexpected delight in Baku's 'unusual' scene is a thriving community of Ultimate Frisbee™ players (the trademark is owned by a leading manufacturer of the flying discs and the game is therefore often known simply as 'Ultimate'). Wikipedia defines the game as "a limited-contact team sport played with a 175 gram flying disc. The object of the game is to score points by passing the disc to a player in the opposing end zone, similar to an end zone in American football or rugby." Baku's co-ed team is called Baku Evil Eyes and meets every Saturday morning, for more information or to join a game, contact them through the Baku Evil Eyes pages on Google groups and Facebook.

Gobustan

info...

Accommodation agencies

There are many agencies offering long and mid-let accommodation rentals in Baku. We recommend Caspian Estates (www.caspianestatesolution.com) who offer a full service, including airport transfers and will even stock your fridge with the basics, help you arrange broadband, local SIM cards and so on.

Addresses

Numbers in addresses refer to the whole building, so up to 6 or more shops and/or doors may share a single address. Sometimes the unit number within the building is given, so 16/2, although that is by no means universal. Many street and building names have changed since Soviet times, with the end result that many people – even taxi-drivers – will not recognise an address, if asked for directions. Note that the Old City Metro is still often known as Baku Soviet Metro, for example, while Fountain Square is rarely recognised, while the old Soviet name of Torgova (Targórva, from the Russian for trade) is used for the square itself and the commercial stretch of Nizami Street nearby. Depressingly, taxi-speak for this area is often also simply 'McDonalds'. The Nasimi district is pretty much universally known simply as Hyatt.

Caviar

There is an export limit of 125g per person, which must still be sealed in factory packing. Be aware when shopping the bazaars that a lot of 'good' deals will be scams. Good caviar can be sourced by the management of Paul's restaurant (see Eat).

Clothing

Young women in Baku wear the skimpiest of outfits in summertime, so it is easy to forget this is a Muslim country. Men in shorts are, however, very much frowned upon, so pack some linen trousers if visiting in the sweltering summer. Outside Baku people are less westernised, so dress appropriately and cover up, especially if visiting religious sites.

Dangers

Baku is an extremely safe city and crime is rare, although the usual precautions should be taken, so avoid flashing your cash. Muggings do occasionally get reported and usually take place near popular Western haunts and down the many badly lit streets. The vast majority of crimes take place when a western male takes home (or to a hotel) one of the girls from one of the insalubrious downtown hook-up joints. Be sensible. If hiking or mountain biking out in the provinces the biggest danger comes from packs of feral dogs, who can normally be deterred by throwing a few stones.

Driving
Other than main thoroughfares, roads are generally appalling, traffic confusing, signage non-existent and driving skills less than amazing. We would strongly advise against self-drive. Cars with drivers can be arranged by either of the travel agencies listed below. If you find a taxi driver who appeals, he will probably be happy to drive for you. Expect to pay in the region of 80-100 US$ per day.

Electricity
Electricity supply is as per continental Europe, so pack a standard Euro travel adaptor.

Internet
Extremely cheap, fast internet cafés are everywhere.

Language
Azeri is very like Turkish and, like Swedes and Norwegians, the Azeris and Turks have a mutual understanding. Anyone over 35 will speak excellent Russian – and a lot of the younger crowd too. Around half of the under 35s will speak some English, but be prepared to be patient and use the international language of smiling and pointing.

Magazines
AZ Magazine – Ex-pat-focused magazine, sign up to get notifications of up and coming events in town – info@az-magazine.com
Boutique Magazine – Russian language style glossy
Impact Magazine – Business-focussed magazine of the American Chamber of

Commerce in Azerbaijan
Visions of Azerbaijan – internationally-focussed magazine published by the European Azerbaijan Society

Money
The Azeri Manat, AZN, is made up of 100 gapiks and is fixed against the dollar, with one dollar buying you 0.8 Manat at any of the many exchange places in town. The sterling rate is not fixed. Credit cards are not universally accepted outside of the hotel chains, so do carry enough cash.

People
70 years of Soviet occupation has left its legacy and many, especially older, people will seem suspicious of interest from a foreigner. While not an obviously smiling populace, Azeris are on the whole very friendly if you make the effort. Younger people are generally more amenable to helping foreigners and will often relish the chance to practice their English.

Photography
Photography is not permitted in the underground or of Presidential buildings. If you ask permission, it will often be denied, but explanation that you are a tourist can end in a good result.

Post
Forget it. The Azeri postal system is highly unreliable. Postcards are all but unavailable and if you can find one, best posted once home. If you require something sent to you in Baku, use a courier service to your hotel.

Pronunciation, spelling & transcription
Consonants are pronounced on the whole as they are in English, with the following principle exceptions. Q is pronounced like an English hard G, so the town of Quba is pronounced Gooba, while the Azeri G is a softer sound – approaching gy. C is pronounced like our J, and S is as pronounced in English. The addition of a tail to these letters is like adding an h in English – Ç = ch and Ş = sh. X is pronounced as in Russian – kh. A final h on a word is pronounced with a guttural sound, as in the Scottish loch.

On the vowel front, things are pretty much as in German, with the addition of two dots above a vowel, prolonging it and flattening it. There are two vowels in Azeri which have no precise equivalent in most European languages. ə is a short vowel and pronounced somewhere between *a* and *e*, like the word cat, and, confusingly, often transcribed as either. For ease, in this guide we have generally transcribed as '*a*'. ı (like *i*, with no dot) is a short *i*, and transcribed here as '*i*' or '*y*'. So the village of *Lahij* is pronounced *Lahij*, a and i are pronounced long, as in *car* and *meet*, while *ey* is pronounced *ay*, as in *bay*, while *ay* is like the *uy* in buy.

Public Transport
The metro is appallingly signed and, with what signage there is being in Azeri only, very tough to navigate. It is, however, very cheap and some stations are very attractive. Buy an oyster card equivalent for 2 AZN, charge it up and each journey will set you back 5 gapiks. Do be sure and count your stops before you board though, as the names of stations are inexplicably not visible from within the carriages when you pull up at a platform. An extremely complicated network of buses and mini-buses also covers the whole city. Trains to elsewhere in Azerbaijan depart from the main station near 28 May Metro, tickets are available from kiosks on the platforms.

Religion
Azerbaijan is about 95% Muslim, with a host of other religions represented in the country and freedom of faith protected by law. In Baku women are rarely scarved and almost never veiled and the free, almost secular nature of Azeri Islam extends to alcohol being freely available and other religions being free to worship.

Taxis
Unlicensed and unmetered, ask how much a journey is and you will often be met with a 'how much do you want to pay'. Most inner city journeys, such as Nasimi district to downtown, should cost no more than 5 AZN. Be aware also that taxi drivers are no better at recognising addresses (see 'Addresses' above) than joe public. If in doubt, check your driver knows where he is going before departure.

Travel Agencies
There are many travel agencies in Baku of varying reliability. We recommend the following, to arrange guided tours around Baku and elsewhere in Azerbaijan, as well as to book English-speaking drivers.
www.improtex-travel.com
www.globaltravel.az

Telephone
Mobile roaming charges in Azerbaijan are astronomical so you may choose to purchase a local SIM from one of the telecomm offices. You will need your passport for this. Azercell is more expensive and has better coverage outside of the city, while Bakcell is cheaper and will suffice if not planning on spending too long in the provinces. Credit can be bought at kiosks on almost every street corner. The country code is +994.

Tipping & taxes
Tipping is welcomed, but by no means expected. 5%-10% of your food bill should

suffice. A VAT rate of 18% is often added to hotel rates. We have quoted where possible with tax included, but be sure and check when booking.

Useful websites
www.news.az - news
www.apa.az - news
www.citylife.az - entertainment listings
www.bakupages.com - news and some entertainment
www.t-e-a-s.eu - The European Azerbaijan Society

Water
Azeri water is not safe to drink, except in hotels. Bottled water is available from cafés and stores city-wide – generally pale blue bottles are still, dark blue are fizzy. Ice cream, ice and water in cafés is usually safe.

Weather
Uniquely, Azerbaijan has nine of the world's eleven possible climates represented in a country only around the size of England. Baku has the unusual distinction of matching the world's average temperature year-round. Very hot in summer; wet in autumn and briefly cold and even snowy in the winter, it is very much like the Mediterranean climate and the best times to visit are late Spring and late Summer. Howling winds come in off the Caspian once or twice a month, so take a wind-proof coat, especially in the European autumn and winter. If visiting the mountains, it can get chilly year-round and extremely cold in the European winter, when some villages and towns are inaccessible due to snowfall.

notes…

index...

Hedonism /hedoniz'm/

"The philosophy that pleasure is the highest
good and proper aim of human life."
– Oxford English Dictionary

Hg2 Corporate

Branded Gifts....

Looking for a corporate gift with real value? Want to reinforce your company's presence at a conference or event? We can provide you with branded guides so recipients will explore their chosen city with your company's logo right under their nose.

Branding can go from a small logo discreetly embossed on to our standard cover, to a fully custom jacket in your company's colours and in a material of your choice. We can also include a letter from your CEO/Chairman/President and add or remove as much or as little other content as you require. We can create a smaller, 'best of' guide, branded with your company's livery in a format of your choice. Custom guides can also be researched and created from scratch to any destination not yet on our list.

For more information, please contact Ben at ben@hg2.com

Content licensing....

We can also populate your own website or other materials with our in-depth content, superb imagery and insider knowledge.

For more information, please contact Tremayne at tremayne@hg2.com

Hg-Who?

Welcome to the world of Hg2 – the UK's leading luxury city guide series. Launched in 2004 as the *A Hedonist's guide to…* series, we are pleased to announce a new look to our guides, now called simply Hg2. In response to customer feedback, the new Hg2 is 25% lighter, even more luxurious to look at or touch, and flexible, for greater portability. However, fear not, our content is still as meticulously researched and well-illustrated as ever and the spirit of hedonism still infuses our work. Our brand of hedonism taps into the spirit of 'Whatever Works for You' – from chic boutique hotels to well-kept-secret restaurants, to the very best cup of coffee in town. We do not mindlessly seek out the most expensive; instead, we search high and low for the very best each city has to offer.

So take Hg2 as your companion to a city. Written by well-regarded journalists and constantly updated online at www.Hg2.com (register this guide to get one year of free access), it will help you Sleep, Eat, Drink, Shop, Party and Play like a sophisticated local.

"Hg2 is about foreign life as art" **Vanity Fair**
"The new travel must-haves" **Daily Telegraph**
"Insight into what's really going on" **Tatler**
"A minor bible" **New York Times**
"Excellent guides for stylish travellers" **Harper's Bazaar**
"Discerning travellers, rejoice!" **Condé Nast Traveller**

Visit Hg2.com now:

Browse the online guide | Read updates | Post reviews | Download city playlists from top DJs | Sign up for special offers | Book Hg2 recommended hotels | Purchase new editions | Play with our interactive maps | Book ready designed trips | Chat in our city forums | Tweet about your experiences And much more…

Our range covers the world's most exciting cities, including:

Almaty & Astana	Marrakech
Baku	Miami
Beirut	Milan
Berlin	Moscow
Buenos Aires	New York
Dubai	Paris
Istanbul	Prague
Lisbon	Rome
London	Stockholm
Los Angeles	Tallinn
Madrid	

All the above are available as books, online and as iPhone apps (www.itunes.com).